Evelyn Wood

Cavalry in the Waterloo Campaign

Evelyn Wood

Cavalry in the Waterloo Campaign

ISBN/EAN: 9783337812157

Printed in Europe, USA, Canada, Australia, Japan

Cover: Foto ©ninafisch / pixelio.de

More available books at **www.hansebooks.com**

THE
Pall Mall Magazine Library

CAVALRY IN THE WATERLOO CAMPAIGN
BY
GENERAL SIR EVELYN WOOD, V.C., &c., &c.

WITH INTRODUCTION
BY
LORD FREDERICK HAMILTON AND SIR DOUGLAS STRAIGHT
EDITORS OF THE "PALL MALL MAGAZINE"

LORD UXBRIDGE, PAINTED AS
HIS EXCELLENCY GENERAL THE MARQUIS OF ANGLESEY, LORD-
LIEUTENANT OF IRELAND, K.G., G.C.B., ETC., ETC.

*After the engraving by Charles Turner, A.R.A., from the painting by
Sir T. Lawrence.*

IN THE

WATERLOO CAMPAIGN

BY

GENERAL SIR EVELYN WOOD, V.C.
&c., &c.

WITH PLANS AND ILLUSTRATIONS

SECOND EDITION

LONDON
SAMPSON LOW, MARSTON, AND COMPANY
LIMITED
St. Dunstan's House
FETTER LANE, FLEET STREET, E.C.
1895

INTRODUCTION.

WHEN the proposal for a series of republications in book form of some of the more important articles and short stories appearing in the pages of the *Pall Mall Magazine* was first made to us by Mr. R. B. Marston, we· accepted it without hesitation, perceiving at once that an admirable medium would thus be provided by which much valuable literary matter might be made known to an even wider circle of the public than the readers of the periodical of which we have the conduct. Field-Marshal Viscount Wolseley's graphic and analytical papers on the "Decline and Fall of Napoleon," which constitute this, the first volume of the PALL MALL MAGAZINE LIBRARY, achieved, as we are able to say from personal knowledge, a very remarkable success not only in England and America, but on the Continent; especially in Paris, where they were translated and published in book form. Much the same may be said with regard to General Lord Roberts' valuable and instructive articles on the "Rise of Wellington," which found especial favour with military readers in all branches of the Service, and we have reason to think that the collection of these into a single and handy volume will meet with the general approval of military men, and might form a valuable text-book for military students. The articles commenced by Viscount Wolseley and continued by Lord Roberts are now being followed in the pages of the *Pall Mall Magazine* by Lieut.-General Sir Evelyn Wood's papers on " Cavalry in the Waterloo Campaign," and we hope from time to time to be able to secure other able military writers as contributors to deal with subjects having an equal historical interest. We conclude by saying that the Publishers have our hearty sympathy and will have our lively co-operation in the publication of the PALL MALL MAGAZINE LIBRARY, and so far as lies in our power we shall endeavour to assist them in making each successive volume such as to entitle it to a foremost place in the literature of the day.

FREDERIC HAMILTON.
DOUGLAS STRAIGHT.
Editors *Pall Mall Magazine.*

18, CHARING CROSS ROAD.
    March, 1895.

PREFACE.

THE publication in the *Pall Mall Magazine* of some papers on the use of Cavalry in the Waterloo Campaign has induced several gentlemen, mostly civilians, to write to me on various points, and from their correspondence it seems that many of my readers who have never served in the Army take deep interest in questions which I had previously thought would only be likely to attract the attention of professional soldiers. It is remarkable that of a party of four with which I revisited Waterloo last year there were two soldiers, one lawyer, and one physician, the two latter being men of admitted reputation in their professions. The knowledge these gentlemen possessed of the campaign was great, and from what I learnt from them and my numerous correspondents I have been induced to enlarge the *Pall Mall Magazine* articles to a greater length than was permissible in the pages of a monthly magazine.

While confining my narrative generally to the operations of the Cavalry, and to the work of the Staff of the Army, so far as it affected the Mounted branches, I have endeavoured, by a study of English, French, and German works, to place before my readers a faithful description of cavalry achievements in the shortest but most decisive campaign of this century.

EVELYN WOOD,
General.

September 30*th,* 1895.

LIST OF SOME OF THE BOOKS USED FOR THE PURPOSE OF THIS NARRATIVE.

Waterloo. By Erckmann-Chatrian.
Campagne de 1815. Par General Gourgaud.
Observations sur la " Relation de la Campagne de 1815." Par le General Grouchy.
Atlas des plus mémorables Batailles, Combats, et Siéges. Par F. von Kausler.
History of the King's German Legion. By Beamish.
Field Services of Cavalry. By Beamish.
Tactics of Cavalry. By Beamish.
The Waterloo Campaign (Arber's). By W. Siborne.
Waterloo Letters. By H. T. Siborne.
Fifteen decisive Battles of the World. By E. S. Creasy.
Histoire de la Campagne de 1815. Par Lieut.-Colonel Charras.
Précis politique et militaire de la Campagne de 1815. Par General Baron de Jomini.
A Voice from Waterloo. By E. Cotton.
Waterloo : the Downfall of the First Napoleon. By George Hooper.
Notes on the Battle of Waterloo. By Sir J. S. Kennedy.
Waterloo Lectures. By Lieut.-Colonel C. C. Chesney.
Fifty Years of my Life. By George Thomas Albemarle.
Geschichte des Feldzuges von 1815. Von General von Ollech.
The War in the Peninsula, and Wellington's Campaigns in France and Belgium. By H. R. Clinton.
Quatre Bras, Ligny, and Waterloo. By Dorsey Gardner.
Histoire de la Campagne de 1815. Par Edgar Quinet.

Words on Wellington. Sir William Fraser.
A Sketch of the Battle of Waterloo. By Baron von Müffling.
Mémoires (1799–1854). Par Marbot.
The Campaign of Waterloo. By J. C. Ropes.
Relation de la Bataille de Mont St. Jean. Par un Témoin Oculaire.
Home's Précis of Modern Tactics.
An Account of the Battle of Waterloo. By Sir Herbert Taylor.
Letters and Journals of Sir W. M. Gomm.
Histoire de la Guerre de la Péninsule sous Napoléon. Par Foy.
Les grands Cavaliers du Premier Empire. Par Thoumas.
De l'Esprit des Institutions de Militaires. Par Marmont.
Souvenirs de Delafosse.
"1815." Par Henry Houssaye.
The Life of Lord Hill.
Revue des deux Mondes, Décembre 1894.
Histoire des deux Restaurations. Par Vaulabelle.
Personal Recollections of Waterloo. By Lieutenant F. H. Pattison, 33rd Regt.
Revue de Cavalerie.
All the Regimental Histories, Cavalry and Infantry, bearing on the Subject.

CONTENTS.

CHAPTER	PAGE
I.—ORGANISATION OF THE FRENCH ARMY	1
II.—THE FRENCH CAVALRY LEADERS, AND HOW THEY CROSSED THE SAMBRE RIVER	28
III.—BATTLE OF LIGNY, 16TH JUNE	51
IV.—QUATRE BRAS AND GENAPPE	66
V.—WATERLOO, 18TH JUNE	110

LIST OF ILLUSTRATIONS.

	PAGE
HIS EXCELLENCY GENERAL THE MARQUIS OF ANGLESEY (LORD UXBRIDGE) .	*Frontispiece*
DIAGRAMS OF FRENCH INFANTRY FORMATIONS IN 1800 AND 1815	7
SKETCH MAP OF THE FRENCH AND BELGIAN FRONTIER IN 1815 . . . . . *To face page*	15
MARSHAL SOULT	18
GENERAL COUNT EXELMANS	31
GENERAL COUNT KELLERMAN	33
FIELD-MARSHAL BLÜCHER	36
SKETCH MAP ILLUSTRATING THE CROSSING OF THE SAMBRE BY THE FRENCH ARMY	39
THE BATTLE OF LIGNY, 16TH JUNE, 1815 . . .	53
BATTLE OF QUATRE BRAS, 16TH JUNE, 1815 . .	67
LORD WELLINGTON	70
GENERAL SIR THOMAS PICTON	74
SKETCH OF COUNTRY NEAR GENAPPE *To face page*	101
NAPOLEON	116

	PAGE
THE BATTLE OF WATERLOO	121
DEFEAT OF D'ERLON'S CORPS AND DUBOIS CAVALRY BRIGADE, BY THE HOUSEHOLD AND UNION BRIGADES . . . . . *To face page*	131
MARSHAL NEY	155
SECTIONS OF THE GROUND OVER WHICH THE FRENCH PASSED TO ATTACK THE RIGHT CENTRE OF THE ALLIES.	157
CHARGE OF THE FRENCH CUIRASSIERS AT WATERLOO	161
WILLIAM PRINCE OF ORANGE	173
DIAGRAM OF THE ATTACK OF VIVIAN'S AND VANDELEUR'S BRIGADES . . . *To face page*	177
FLIGHT FROM WATERLOO	185

CAVALRY

IN THE

WATERLOO CAMPAIGN.

CHAPTER I.

ORGANISATION OF THE FRENCH ARMY.

"And that it was great pity, so it was,
That villainous saltpetre should be digg'd
Out of the bowels of the harmless earth,
Which many a good tall fellow had destroyed
So cowardly;"
KING HENRY IV., Act I., Scene iii.

UNTIL the use of firearms became general, Horsemen had but little to fear from Infantry, but since Hotspur thus related the lament of the "popinjay lord" there have been to the present day progressive improvements in "cowardly" weapons, and we now possess a rifle which, when fired horizontally on level ground, propels a bullet through the air for five hundred yards without its rising more than five feet, or the height of a boy's head.

The announcement of each improvement in firearms since the days of "Brown Bess," has been accompanied with the confident assertion by many infantry soldiers, based mainly on results of rifle-range practices, that the days of cavalry have passed away. It is probable, however, that these Soldier-prophets have either never seen Cavalry properly led, or never studied closely what that Arm of the Service has achieved. We find all the great Continental Powers are increasing the number of their mounted troops, while the most successful "Nation in Arms," believing thoroughly in the use of shock tactics, has adopted the lance, not only for "Medium," but also for "Light" Cavalry, and, as I think unwisely, for Hussars, who are too short to wield a lance effectively. Although three years ago Russia, to the astonishment of military students, decided to turn great numbers of its Cavalry into Mounted Infantry, it appears that this decision has already been abandoned. Moreover though the Great Powers have every reason to economise, yet since the war of 1870–71 they have continued to add cavalry to their armies, and to train it with still greater care. Now, as cavalry takes three times as long to train, and is three times more costly to maintain than infantry, it is obvious that on the Continent, at least, it is not believed that "the age of chivalry has passed away at last."*

My main reasons for believing in the Continental views rather than in those of some of my comrades are:—

Firstly.—Because the conditions under which rifle practice is executed in peace and war differ so materially as to furnish but unreliable data on which to base deductions of any value. On the Rifle ranges, soldiers practise with every advantage that health, good-living, fair weather, and light equipment can give. They never fire when fatigued, since Commanding Officers object to their men being marched more than about four miles to a range. And they never shoot in unfavourable weather, for fear of their losing the monetary prizes which are granted for proficiency in these exercises. Nevertheless, on service, Infantry may often be called on to withstand Cavalry, when exhausted by long marches, want of food, and while encumbered by equipment which must militate against good shooting.

Secondly.—Though weapons are improved yearly, the human heart remains the same. Discipline enhances its military value, but then thorough discipline

* Old song, by Mrs. Norton.

cannot be acquired in a few months, and with the immense growth of armies, the time the infantry soldier is kept under training has been so reduced that it is possible this, or the coming generation, may see a repetition of glorious cavalry achievements such as astonished the world eighty years ago.

Many authors have written on the Waterloo campaign, but no one has, so far as I am aware, brought out fully and consecutively the operations of the Mounted branches of the Army during the four days' fighting. It is to these, and to the Leaders and Staff directing the Mounted branches, that I propose to confine my story, telling sufficient only of the general operations to render my narrative intelligible. I shall endeavour to show when, and under what conditions, cavalry attacks succeeded and failed, in order that my readers may judge how far they are likely to be successful in the future. To form accurate opinions we must however consider the efficiency of the contending forces.

Some French and many English historians of this campaign describe Napoleon's Army as being "the finest he had ever commanded." This assertion has no foundation in fact, except as regards the stature of the old soldiers; and to so term them on this ground is as reasonable as to assert that eight old "Dark" or

"Light Blues," who had formerly rowed in the winning boat of different years, could, when hurriedly brought together for the first time in their lives, form the finest crew ever sent by the Universities to the Thames. Moreover, the old soldiers who had returned in 1814, from captivity in foreign lands, formed only a part of Napoleon's forces, amongst which were many young and immature men. About 50 per centum of the Line were recruits, and of the Imperial Guard, 18,500 strong, between 4000 and 5000 were untrained men.

The formations employed during the first Empire indicate clearly the gradual decline of the French Infantry in military efficiency, as the waste in the ranks was made up by drafts of younger and less trained men. But it was not only the men in the Ranks who were less efficient. The great development of the Army, and its losses in action, had enabled many men to become company and battalion commanders who were unfitted for such posts. Thus battalions could no longer be successfully employed when fighting away from the supervision of superior officers. When the Generals realised that their battalions could not be trusted in extended formations, they gradually increased the depth of columns, losing thereby the advantages of fire action and manœuvring power. Jomini describes how, against insufficiently trained troops, the moral effect of massive columns often caused defenders to abandon a position without awaiting an attack. When, however, such formations were employed against British infantry drawn up in line they failed, for the leading ranks, on being struck by a shower of bullets, invariably faltered, and tried to deploy, as happened both at Quatre Bras, and at Waterloo. The diagrams on the opposite page indicate clearly that the French infantry which fought so bravely at Waterloo was not, in the opinion of its Leaders, the most efficient which Napoleon commanded during his glorious career.

There were, moreover, other reasons militating against efficiency amongst the Rank and File. In the Spring of 1814 there were 180,000 cases of desertion in two months, and during the ensuing summer the following reductions were carried out, to the serious discontent of the many officers placed in retirement: infantry, from 206 to 107 regiments; cavalry, from 99 to 61 regiments; artillery, from 339 to 184 batteries. On April 1st, 1815, the paper strength of the army in France was 190,000, it having been increased some 40,000 in the latter part of 1814. From all these changes it is clear that the Regimental officers could not have had that intimate knowledge of their men's character which is essential for success.

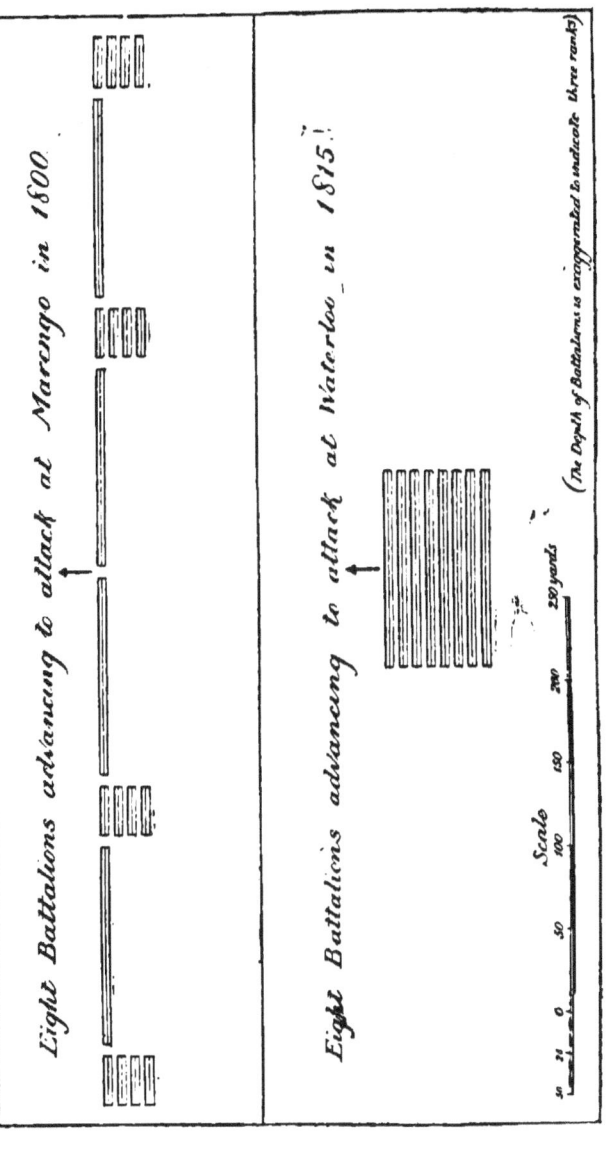

Many Regimental officers also were discontented, and from a variety of causes. During the Restoration bribery was prevalent. Honours and Titles were sold at recognised prices, the Legion of Honour being valued at from 250 to 300 francs, and in the five months from August to December 1814 more decorations were granted than in the whole of the preceding twelve years of the Empire. In the same period of 1814 there were more patents of Nobility issued than in the last 200 years of the Monarchy of France! With Napoleon's return many of these nominations were cancelled, between 2000 and 3000 being recalled; and whereas the Bonapartists had been at first disgusted at the cheapening of the previously hardly-earned Legion of Honour, those from whom it was now retaken were on their part aggrieved.

It may be easier for my civilian readers to comprehend the strength and weakness of Napoleon's army as a fighting machine if I show briefly the steps taken to reorganise it, and what happened between the 1st March and the opening of the campaign. Napoleon, having disembarked in the Gulf of St. Juan on the 1st March, left the coast on the 2nd March, 1815, with one weak battalion, General Cambronne with forty Grenadiers moving in front of him, as an advanced guard. When this advanced guard came face to face with the 5th Regiment near Vizelle, Napoleon ordered his men to "Secure" arms, and dismounted from his horse. It was a critical moment for his fortunes, but he walked up to the Royal battalion, 700 strong, drawn up to oppose him, and having saluted it exclaimed: "If any soldier wants to shoot his General, who is also his Emperor, here I am!" For a moment there was an intense silence, and then there arose a mighty shout, "Long live the Emperor," and the soldiers on either side fraternised.

There can be no doubt of the enthusiasm felt for him, not only in the army, but in certain sections of the country. At a review held on the 16th April, 1815, he stood practically alone, although he had received many warnings of officers and others having left La Vendee in order to assassinate him. Disregarding all these threats he had but one unarmed grenadier by his side, whose duty it was to receive petitions, and a woman coming out of the crowd handed the Emperor a paper. Napoleon, imagining it to be a request for help, passed it to the orderly, that he might read it at his leisure, but on re-entering his apartments, he found that the unknown woman had given him £800!!

That Napoleon appreciated accurately the feeling

in the Army, is clear from the following memoranda dictated at St. Helena:—

"I owed my restoration to the inhabitants of the towns and villages, to the soldiers, and junior company officers. I could rely only on them. All the generals I met on my journey hesitated, or received me badly even if they were not hostile, but they were obliged to give way before the excitement of their soldiers. Marshal Macdonald and General St. Cyr endeavoured to keep their troops loyal to the Government, and the attempt nearly cost them their lives."

Many of the senior officers, though young in years, had become heavy, gross in body, and incapable of much exertion, and Napoleon realised, though too late, that he should have put the commands into the hands of younger men. This slackness on the part of the senior officers had become apparent during the later campaigns in Germany, for at Leipsic, Napoleon, through a field glass, observed one of his Marshals riding up to join his troops after they had been several hours engaged.

Napoleon entered Paris on the 21st March, having had, after the first week of his disembarkation, a triumphant march. He at once set to work in re-organising the army, and, as regards the mounted branches especially, the task was stupendous.

Owing to the second deposition of Napoleon and the entire dissolution of his army, there are very few Regimental details in French accounts of this reorganisation, and of the events of June 15th—19th, 1815; but my Cavalry readers will appreciate the immense difficulties under which Napoleon's mounted troops laboured, when they reflect that, of 187,600 horses which crossed the Niemen in 1812, only 1600 came back! These appalling losses were nearly all due to starvation and unripe food; and during the retreat, officers who still owned horses were formed into squadrons 150 strong, which were commanded by General officers, Colonels acting as non-commissioned officers. One of the regiments (4^{ieme} Lanciers) engaged on June 16th, 1815, went to Russia 600 strong, but returned with only one officer and 17 Rank and File! Students of history will remember how short of cavalry Napoleon was at Lützen in 1813, when most of the regiments had but two squadrons; and after the losses suffered in the disastrous autumn campaign of that year, the cavalry was freely used in the short but brilliant campaign of 1814. Thoumas mentions the moral effect produced amongst the squads of boy recruits then enrolled in the ranks by the arrival of trained cavalry soldiers from Spain.

On Napoleon's departure for Elba, in April 1814,

the titles of the regiments were changed, as wer many officers: the sixty-one regiments remainin after the reduction being each brought down to thre weak squadrons. In December there was a furthe reorganisation—several ex-prisoners of war, and othe1, called in from furlough, replacing men till then in th ranks.

The decree of the 28th March, recalling to the arm all non-commissioned officers and privates who ha been discharged for whatever reason, was not issue till fifteen days after it was signed, Napoleon fearin to alarm the peasantry; and soon after the 9th Apri the day on which it was published, the Public fund fell, a feeling of discouragement becoming prevalen throughout the country. The peasantry, who had bee rejoicing at the abolition by the Emperor of som vexatious taxes, now began to fear that his retur would cause possibly an invasion, but certainly war. This idea was so unpopular, that many of th soldiers, even including those who had served unde Napoleon, failed to obey the summons to rejoi Although a great many of those who deserted in 181 gave as a reason that they would not wear th Bourbon colours, yet several had quitted the arm from dislike of war, which it must be remembered ha been latterly, almost without exception, unfortunate

In spite of this feeling however, during the first week in June, 52,000 old soldiers had actually joined, and 23,000 more had left their homes to report themselves at their respective stations. In calling up the conscripts for the year 1815, the Emperor got 20,000 who had served in 1814, they having been previously conscripted one year in anticipation of their time.

The Emperor found that the two mounted Arms of the service consisted of nothing more than depôts without horses or guns, and that the arsenals contained no spare muskets. The army numbered in all but 190,000 men of all branches of the service with 35,000 horses.

Napoleon collected men more quickly than he could manufacture arms and equipment, of which there was a great deficiency. In twenty regiments men had no boots or shoes, and in even the *Corps d'elite*, the supply was inadequate. Up to the 12th June, the Imperial Guard, and the five Corps d'Armée which were intended to invade Belgium, with few exceptions, had not a second pair of boots, and the last of the equipment for the mounted troops was not issued till the end of May.

On the 20th March, there were only 28,000 horses in the cavalry, and the artillery and train had but 8000 on paper, of which 5000 had been let out to farmers. Half the mounted gendarmery were then ordered to send in their horses, each man receiving 600 francs in payment, and by this means 4300 horses were obtained, and distributed among the Cuirassier and Dragoon regiments. The General who was put in charge of the Remount dépôt at Versailles did not understand his business, for he declined to accept any horses over age, and even if they were half an inch under the regulated height ; but nevertheless Napoleon managed to collect 41,000 horses for the cavalry, and some 16,000 for artillery and transport purposes.

That Napoleon could in two months collect 20,000 horsemen for his invasion of Belgium, after providing for the Army Corps guarding the other frontiers of France, and having had a nucleus of 8000 horses only on which to start the mobilisation, is one of the many proofs of his marvellous genius ; but the inevitable hurry, and consequent want of training, accounts in a great measure for the want of success attained by the French Cavalry, notwithstanding the heroic conduct displayed by many individuals, who freely offered their lives to make up for the want of training of their regiments. Those who have had to train large drafts of recruits brought suddenly into a regiment previously in a high state of efficiency must,

if they know the facts, feel astonished not only at what Napoleon expected of his untrained horsemen, but at what they actually accomplished. The many decrees issued by the Emperor during the "Hundred days," and their nature, indicate his difficulties in raising men. That dated March 28th, brought alongside boyish recruits, old men of sixty years of age, some of whom it is said had served in the Italian campaigns, when Napoleon was Consul.

On the 1st June, 1815, the effectives reached 217,000, of which there were available for the Waterloo campaign, 115,000, composed of 86,000 infantry, 20,000 cavalry, 7000 artillery, and 2000 sappers.

Napoleon left Paris at 3 A.M. on the 12th June, the Guards having set out on the 5th. On the 14th, the French army was concentrated at Maubeuge, Beaumont, and Philippeville. Headquarters were at Beaumont. At these three places the troops were all encamped under cover of low hills within a few miles of the frontier, being so well placed that the enemy remained unaware of the proximity of the large masses of troops.

Cavalry divisions, about 1500 strong, were attached to the corps as follows :—

To the 1st Corps (Count D'Erlon's), the division commanded by General Jacquinot.

To the 2nd Corps (Count Reille's), the division commanded by General Piré.

To the 3rd Corps (Count Vandamme's), the division commanded by General Domon.

To the 4th Corps (Count Gérard's), the division commanded by General Maurin.

The Reserve of cavalry under supreme command of General Grouchy was thus divided :—

    1st Cavalry Corps, Count Pajol.
    2nd   „   „   Count Exelmans.
    3rd   „   „   Count Kellerman.
    4th   „   „   Count Milhaud.

Each of these consisted of some 2600 sabres, with two batteries of artillery attached.

The Young Guard was formed of volunteers and the men called back to the colours who had previously served in the Young Guard. For the Middle Guard, the men for the artillery and cavalry were taken from the gendarmery and the line, each regiment of which had to supply fifty selected men, with a minimum of eight years' service, and those drafted into the infantry were required to be of four years' service.

On the evening of the 14th, 115,000 men answered the Roll call, and there were 350 guns present. Napoleon on the morning of the 14th issued a stirring "order of the day" to his army, in the concluding sentences of which he called on every man "to conquer or die in the attempt." This spirit animated most of the old soldiers in the ranks, but the same exalted feeling was not shared by the generals, several of whom, though young in years, were prematurely aged, and such had lost that determined audacity which had gained so many battles under the Republic and the Empire.

All of them, Soult, Ney, Grouchy, Grouet, Lobau, Kellerman, Vandamme, Bachelu, Gérard, Druot, Exelmans, and Foy, were between forty and fifty years of age. Unfortunately for Napoleon, most of them no longer believed that the Emperor could succeed; and possibly his own confidence in his Star was no longer what it had been.

Ney, Lobau, and many others felt that they were not only risking their lives in battle, but that unless Napoleon succeeded in maintaining his throne they would probably be tried by Court martial and shot. Gérard, Exelmans, and Vandamme, however, were full of zeal and confidence. The two latter were not on speaking terms with Soult, who had certainly treated Exelmans ungenerously, and though he did not allow the incident to affect his conduct, yet it must have impaired Soult's influence and I therefore will tell the story briefly.

When Murat was reinstated by the Allied Sovereigns as King of Naples, Exelmans wrote a friendly letter to his former Chief with whom he had served as Aide-de-camp in Italy, and in Germany in 1805. This letter, being intercepted in the post, was put

SOULT.

before Louis XVIII., who contented himself wit desiring the Minister of War to request Exelmans t be more guarded in future. This did not satisf Soult, and although Countess Exelmans was about t be confined, Soult ordered him to leave Paris imm diately. Exelmans refused, and when a general officer was sent with a picquet of soldiers to take him prisoner, he threatened to kill the first man who laid a hand on him. This threat was successful.

The Countess having appealed to the Chamber of Deputies, the appeal was accepted, and by a Royal decree the General was ordered to be tried before a court-martial at Lille, but was unanimously acquitted.

Soult and Exelmans did not meet again till the 16th June, 1815, when Grouchy, having sent for Exelmans, began to talk to him in Soult's presence. The Marshal in the first instance bent his eyes down on a map, but seeing it was impossible to ignore his presence, eventually held out his hand, saying, "How are you?" Exelmans shook his hand, but the quarrel between them was not made up.

Soult's relations with Vandamme were not friendly. I do not wish it to be understood that I imply this was Soult's fault; for Vandamme, although brave to the last degree, was not only impetuous and hasty, but rough-mannered, and one with whom it was difficult to preserve amicable relations. Count Ferenzac narrates that in Germany he insulted grievously the Prince of Eckmühl (Davout), who was very much mortified, but bearing in mind a message he had just received from Napoleon saying, "Try to manage Vandamme, there are few soldiers like him on service," he put up with his junior officer's insubordination.

On the evening of the 14th June, when an officer was sent with an order for Vandamme to advance with his corps at 3 A.M., the General could not be found. He had gone off to a house at some distance from his corps, and had not left word where he was sleeping. The orderly officer, who wandered about during the night endeavouring to find the General, eventually fell from his horse and broke his leg. He lay helpless for some time, and thus the order was never delivered to Vandamme, who started only at seven o'clock instead of three in the morning.

On the afternoon of the 15th, when Napoleon decided to give Ney and Grouchy the commands of the two wings of his forces, Soult omitted to inform Vandamme that he was to pass under Grouchy' orders, and when later Grouchy ordered him to advance and press the retreat of the Prussians Vandamme refused to take orders from him.

The late Colonel Home in his admirable 'Preci of Modern Tactics,' quoting von Hardegg, says that "If the General may be regarded as representing the head of a human body, the Staff may be justl compared to the nerves which convey the volition from the head to the different members," and it is obvious that in order to obtain the best results, those conveying the orders of the Chief should work in unison with all the members of the body.

The appointment of Marshal Soult to act as Chief of the Staff has been often criticised as an unfortunate selection, but Napoleon had little choice, and he appears in all the appointments he made to have done his best for the army. He promoted to be General, Colonel Cuneo d'Ornano, who had imprisoned five-and-twenty of Napoleon's escort when he landed near Cannes, and speaking generally, Napoleon, after his return, never resented the conduct of anyone who had acted according to duty. Perhaps the strongest case was that of General Rapp. Napoleon said to him, "Would you have dared to have fired on me?" Rapp replied, "Certainly, because it was my duty!" and Napoleon gave him command of the army assembling on the Rhine!

Nearly all French authors ascribe the delay in sending out orders to the incapacity of Marshal Soult as Chief of the Staff. Colonel Chesney does not accept this view, attributing many mistakes to Napoleon, and has no difficulty in pointing out many inconsistent passages in the memoirs dictated at St. Helena; but all officers who have served on the Staff, and in command, will admit that after serving some years as Head of a force, a man is less able to bend his mind to work out in detail the conceptions of another Chief. Moreover, the junior Staff officers, assembled in a hurry, were unaccustomed to work in concert.

Soult was suspected by the friends of the Legitimists, by the Bonapartists, and also by the Liberals, and was detested by many of the officers. The choice of Chief of the Staff was a great trouble to Napoleon, and Berthier was greatly missed. The latter was neither a great General, nor an organiser, nor a man of great ability, but he was an admirable Staff officer to Napoleon—indefatigable, comprehensive, diligent, quick to comprehend the most complicated orders, and very clever in elaborating them with the necessary precision and exactitude. For nineteen years he served Napoleon admirably. He had been at Ghent for a short time, but was at Bamberg when Napoleon returned from Elba. He attempted to re-enter France, but on coming across one of the Allied armies, he turned back. On the afternoon of the 10th June, as a regiment of Russian Dragoons passed his house, on their way to France, Berthier suddenly left the window of the first floor, from which he had been looking out, and running upstairs to the room occupied by his children on the third floor, threw himself out of the window, and was picked up dead.

The desertion of General Bourmont, the General commanding the leading division, together with his personal Staff, exercised an unfavourable effect on the French troops, and should therefore be mentioned He began his career as chief of the Royalist troops in the West of France. Being taken into the Imperial service, he had distinguished himself in several campaigns; but Napoleon, suspecting his loyalty, refused in the first instance to employ him during the "Hundred days," and consented only to do so on General Gérard declaring that he would be personally responsible for him. On the morning of the 15th June, Bourmont was with the leading (3rd) division of Gérard's corps, which had lain overnight at Florenne, a village six miles North of Philippeville.

At 5.30 A.M.. the General rode forward in front of his division as if to reconnoitre the road, accompanied by two Staff officers and three Aides-de-camp, and attended by a corporal and six orderlies. Having sent away two of the orderlies, the General then had six men against five, whom he ordered back, giving the corporal two letters for General Gérard. It is doubtful whether General Bourmont gave the Prussians Napoleon's plan, which he had received the previous evening, but there cannot be any doubt that Blücher's Staff gained from him information which would not otherwise have reached them for several hours.

The French soldiers were furious at this desertion, and they suspected many of the other generals as being capable of similar conduct. During the battle of the 16th, an old corporal of the Guard went up to the Emperor near St. Amand, and said, "Your Majesty, don't you trust Marshal Soult, it is quite certain he will betray us." Again in the evening of that day, when the first officers reported to Vandamme that an unknown column was in sight, he galloped off to reconnoitre, and one of his Staff riding up to Soult reported that his general had deserted. This induced the soldiers around to shout out that the Emperor should be warned! The soldiers really thought that they had been deceived by the Staff, and that not one general only, but a dozen, had gone over to the enemy.

The question of how much troops should be told, or how far hoodwinked, has often been discussed.

We read that when Count Gneisenau was begged to send reinforcements into Ligny on the 16th June, that he answered at 8 P.M., " Hold the village for only half-an-hour more, for we expect the English troops to arrive every minute!" and yet we know from Muffling's memoirs that soon after Wellington returned from his interview with Blücher to Quatre Bras, Muffling sent to Gneisenau to say that it would be impossible for Wellington, who was heavily engaged, to render any assistance to the Prussians.

This may have deceived the overmatched Prussians but there is no doubt that in the Waterloo campaign the French soldiers disbelieved everything which was not confirmed by their own eyesight. Nor is this difficult of explanation since the Emperor had never hesitated in giving such colouring to his reports as he thought would best affect the object he had immediately in view. Perhaps the most striking instance of his reckless disregard of the truth, is that during the last struggle on the 18th June, 1815; he sent his Aide-de-camp, Labedoyère, to pass down from Right to Left of the attacking columns, and assure the generals that the sound of the firing heard on the extreme right and right-rear of the French position was caused by the advance of Grouchy, whereas it was in reality the outcome of a desperate struggle between the 6th Corps (Lobau's) and the advancing Prussians of Von Bulow's (4th) corps.

Marshal Ney bitterly resented this deception,

which he stigmatised later in the plainest terms. He had marched into Paris on March 23rd, 1815, with troops sent out to arrest the progress of Napoleon, but which eventually passed under his orders. Ney had made a foolish boast to the Legitimist Government that "he would bring Bonaparte back in an iron cage to Paris." The Emperor, his former master, was magnanimous enough to disregard this bombastic observation, and sent his former right-hand fighting man into the Departments of the North of France, ostensibly to report on the fortresses, but in reality to furnish detailed reports on the opinions and intentions of all the functionaries, military and civil. Ney carried this out to the best of his ability, but his humble origin and want of breeding militated greatly against success. He disgusted alike Royalists and Imperialists by the coarse, vulgar expressions he used in his conversation regarding the Government he had recently served, speaking habitually of the Bourbons as "a rotten lot." Neither did this conduct re-establish Ney in the confidence of the Bonapartists, who wrote anonymously advising the Emperor not to employ him.

When the Marshal returned about the 15th April from his tour in the Northern Departments, he tried to excuse to the Emperor the bombastic boast he had made to the King. He alleged that he had already determined to go over to his former Chief, and that the boast was a mere blind. Napoleon received this incredible assertion in silence, and Ney retired to his country seat. When he next saw the Emperor at the "Champ de Mai" parade, Napoleon said, "What, you here! I thought you had emigrated." Ney answered bitterly, "I ought to have done so sooner."

It is supposed that the Emperor felt some personal regret for one who had served so long under him, and also realised that a great battle without Ney would be shorn of its greatest fighting factor, so he sent for him on the 11th June. The Marshal, hastily borrowing some money from friends, posted to the Front, and dined with the Emperor at Avesnes On the 13th he was fortunate in finding horses which he purchased from a brother Marshal (Mortier) who was taken ill on the frontier; but when, late in the afternoon of the 15th, he took over the command of the left wing of the army (1st and 2nd Army Corps) he had no Staff, nor did he even know the names of the General Officers commanding divisions.

CHAPTER II.

THE FRENCH CAVALRY LEADERS, AND HOW THEY CROSSED THE SAMBRE RIVER.

MARSHAL MARMONT, in his 'De l'Esprit des Institutions de Militaires,' points out the great difficulty in obtaining an able leader of cavalry, because the qualities which produce a good horse-master are apt to render him chary of sacrificing his horses at the critical moment. Marmont writes, " Up to the evening of the battle in which the cavalry are called to fight, the General should exercise, over men and horses, the most minute care and attention. He should watch over their efficiency with the greatest solicitude, but at the moment of action should be capable of expending them without a thought of the losses he may be about to incur, being dominated by the sole idea of getting as much out of them as possible." The Marshal enlarges on the almost impossibility of finding any one man with these two opposite qualifications.

Everyone admits the great influence exercised by

an efficient cavalry leader over the best-drilled troops, but with undisciplined levies hastily brought together for the first time the personal characteristics and influence exerted by a leader are even more important. The four French cavalry leaders who distinguished themselves in the four days' fighting, were, Counts Pajol, Milhaud, Exelmans and Kellerman.

Count Pajol.—This officer, who had graduated in his military career under Kléber, Richepanse, and Ney, was the best type of a "Light cavalry" general. Always at the head of his men, he was seven times wounded, three times in hand-to-hand fighting; and between his first campaign at the passage of the Lahn in 1795, and that of 1815, twelve horses were killed under him at different times. One of his wounds was received in seizing with his own hands a colour from the enemy, and at Wagram he grappled with a colonel of an opposing regiment, and pulling him off his horse made him a prisoner.*

Count Milhaud.—Milhaud was one of those brave cavalry generals whose courage helped to gain so many battles for Napoleon, but the last acts of his career show him to have been wanting in force of character, for he stooped to make friends with the

* I am indebted mainly to General Thoumas' 'Grand Cavaliers' for the biographies of these four leaders.

Bourbon Government, in a way that many of his comrades declined to do. This was the more despicable since he had voted for the execution of Louis XVI., and yet, after Waterloo, he boasted to the Legitimist Government of "his love for the ancient and sacred race of the kings of France." If we except this unsatisfactory record of his life, all the rest, and especially that which had to do with battles, is much in his favour. Before the campaign of 1815, he had proved himself to be one of the best cavalry leaders in the Grand Army. In 1796, charging at the head of six squadrons, he took three thousand prisoners, and eight guns. He commanded a Light cavalry brigade in 1805 and 1806, and was at the head of a Division of dragoons in Spain, and again at the battle of Wachau, and in the fatal campaign of 1814. Perhaps his reputation was highest at the battle of Ocaña, where he had an astounding success against the Spanish cavalry. The most severe of all the critics of that epoch, Marmont, Duke of Raguse, who was eight years younger than Milhaud, speaks slightingly of him as "an old Radical," but admits that he was a good comrade, and a brave soldier. To go through the rest of his services would necessitate mentioning nearly all the numerous campaigns which Napoleon's army waged.

Count Exelmans.—In 1791, at the age of sixteen,

he entered a company of artillery, attached to an infantry regiment, and was still a lieutenant eight years afterwards, when at the head of six grenadiers

GENERAL EXELMANS.

of the 64th regiment, he successfully stormed the walls of Trani after the grenadiers of the regiment had been beaten back. In 1799, he was for this feat made captain in the 16th Dragoon Regiment, and from that time on he continued to distinguish himself on every occasion in which he met the enemy. When serving in Italy he killed the officer commanding a regiment, and took ten of the men prisoners with his own hands. At the age of twenty-eight he was still, however, only a squadron leader. He was acting as Aide-de-camp to Murat, when by chance he came on the 9th Dragoon Regiment engaged in the village of Wertingen. If the French troops which shortly before had surprised the enemy, had gone on at once, they might have captured the Austrian officers at breakfast, in the village, but the leading squadron, being met by a heavy fire, halted until Exelmans passed the spot while carrying a message. He, calling on the colonel to dismount one hundred and fifty men, got off himself, and with them captured the village. Remounting the men he led them on, followed by the remainder of the regiment, which charged an Austrian square formed of nine battalions; the colonel and the second-in-command, who rode on his right and left, were wounded, and Exelmans' horse, in pain from a bayonet wound, threw him over its head. He must have been killed but that Lannes and Murat, attracted by the firing, came up, and a few days later Exelmans was sent with the Stand of colours taken from the enemy to the Emperor at Donauwœrth on the Danube, who received him with the expression, " I know very well there is no braver man in the army than thou." From this time forth Exelmans fought

KELLERMAN.

in every campaign in Germany and distinguished himself particularly at the Katzbach, Wachau, Leipsic, and in the battles of 1814.

Kellerman.—François - Etienne de Kellerman, a son of the victor of Valmy, was born in 1770, and entered the army as a sub-lieutenant in 1785. Five years later he went to New York with the apparent intention of becoming a diplomatist, for which he had many qualifications, as he proved in conducting the Cintra Convention, but doubtless the main reason was that he feared his feeble state of health might impede his career in the army. He returned to Europe, however, three years later, and distinguished himself first of all at the crossing of the Tagliamento, where, when acting as a Staff officer, he put himself at the head of two cavalry regiments and rode over several Austrian squadrons, taking five guns. His next notable feat was in Italy, near Nepi, where, being in command of an advanced guard of three squadrons, two guns, and two battalions of Infantry, he attacked 8000 Neapolitans with such vigour as to rout them with a loss of 500 killed and wounded. In another place I shall describe at length his brilliant achievement at Marengo.

It is probable that the enemies of the Emperor always made the worst of any sign of weakness shown by that greatest of modern Generals, but there can be no doubt that Napoleon was, in the first instance at all events, annoyed by the victory on the 14th June, 1800, being attributed mainly to Desaix and to Kellerman. It is probable that Kellerman talked too much of what he had done, and an i cautious letter which he wrote to his friend Lasalle, then in Paris, and which fell into the hands of Napoleon, who controlled the Post office entirely, increased the First Consul's irritation. In this letter Kellerman wrote : "What do you think, my friend? Bonaparte has not made me a General! Me! who have just put the crown of France on his head." At Austerlitz, Kellerman covered himself with glory in his repeated charges; two of his Staff officers were killed or wounded, one on each side of him, and he himself had his leg broken by a musket shot. He was again wounded when commanding a brigade at Lützen, but recovered in time to lead the cavalry of an army corps at the battle of Bautzen. Justice compels me to admit that his financial methods startled even the soldiers of his age, some of whom in such matters were not easily shocked, but as a leader of cavalry he was superb.

On June 13th and 14th, 1815, the Allied armies stretched over a Front of nearly a hundred miles, from Namur on the Meuse, to the Scheldt, and with a depth from Front to Rear, in many places, of forty miles. The armies joined on the Charleroi-Brussels road; the Prussians, who were generally nearer the frontier, being supplied from the Rhine, through

Liège and Maestricht, and the English through Ostend and Antwerp.

The Prussians numbered 113,000 infantry, with 12,000 cavalry, and 312 guns, being divided into four

BLÜCHER.

Corps, which, reckoning from East to West, stood a follows: Bulow near Liège, Thielmann near Ciney Pirch at Namur, and Ziethen about Charleroi, th Headquarters under Marshal Blücher being at Namu A considerable proportion of this army consisted o militia, and there was a large per centum of recruits in the ranks of the line regiments.

The Duke of Wellington commanded 106,000 in all, of which 27,000 infantry, 8000 cavalry, and 5500 gunners manning 120 guns, were British or German Legion, while the remainder belonged to different nations. He had his Headquarters and the Reserve division under Picton at Brussels, and also a division of Brunswick troops, and a Nassau brigade.

The 1st Corps, led by the Prince of Orange, was composed of the 1st and 3rd British divisions, with some Dutch and Belgian troops; the 2nd Corps, under Lord Hill, was composed of the 2nd and 4th British divisions, and a contingent of Dutch and Belgians. The Prince of Orange's troops were extended over the line Nivelles, Enghien and Mons, and the 2nd Corps was between the latter fortified city and the sea.

By a series of skilfully combined and rapidly executed movements, the six French Army Corps were concentrated on the 13th and 14th June behind a line of wooded hills called "the forest of Mormal," the right being at Philippeville, the centre and Headquarters at Beaumont, and the left at Sol-sur-Sambre. This river, which rises in France, is navigable from Landrecis downwards for about a hundred miles, till it falls into the Meuse, and is passable only at the bridges.

During the night of the 13th the red light reflected in the sky by the fire of the enemy's bivouacs, was reported by Zieten's outposts, the light being most visible in the direction of Beaumont and Sol-sur-Sambre, and on the 14th there was ample information of the immediate advance, brought over the frontier by country people, who were driving their cattle away for safety. Zieten was told to await in position the attack, and then fall back when necessary, on Fleurus. His 1st brigade was around Fontaine l'Eveque: the 2nd in Marchiennes and Gilly: the 3rd in Fleurus: the 4th near Namur: the reserve cavalry about Gosselies.

During the night, 14th–15th, trusted French agents, leaving Brussels, reached Napoleon's Headquarters with the welcome news that, up to the evening of the 14th, no orders had been issued for the concentration of Wellington's army.

In pursuance of the orders issued by the Emperor, Count Pajol's cavalry corps, at 2.30 A.M., on the 15th June, having on its left Domon's division, moved from its bivouac North of Beaumont, on Charleroi. It was intended that Vandamme with the 3rd Corps should follow close behind the cavalry, but owing, as

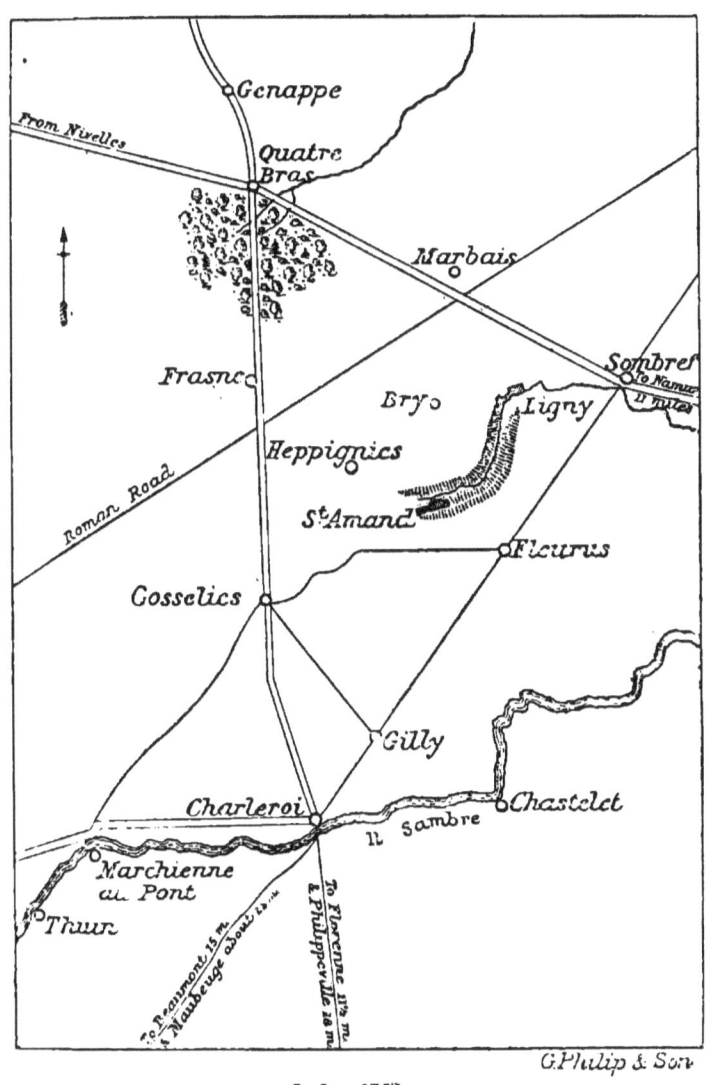

I have shown,* to the orders not having reached that General, his corps did not start till 7 A.M., thus delaying also the Imperial Guard which was to follow on the same road.

At 6 A.M. in the morning Pajol's leading regiment came on a Prussian battalion which had barricaded the road near the village of Ham-sur-Heure. Pajol sent his leading brigade at the defenders of the barricade, who fled, leaving about one hundred prisoners in the hands of the French. The cavalry corps then moved on Charleroi. After it rejoined Domon's division, its leading regiments came on some detachments of the enemy which had collected in the farmhouse called La Tombe. Pajol sent the 4th and 9th Chasseurs to attack the farm, but mounted men could produce no effect in its enclosures until the General, bringing up a howitzer, opened fire, when between two and three hundred Prussians surrendered.

Count Pajol's horsemen now felt the want of infantry support, but they continued the march in order to keep up with the heads of General Reille's (2nd) Corps, which were now attacking Marchiennes-au-Pont.

Soult's† division arrived at the river at 8.30 A.M., and Pajol sent him forward, but the cavalry were

* Page 20.   † Brother of the Chief of the Staff.

driven back by the heavy fire of a number of troops in skirmishing order who were concealed behind the hedges and in the Southernmost houses of the village. The Count, while waiting for Vandamme, looked, but in vain, for fords by which he might cross to the other side of the river.

While the cavalry divisions were waiting for Vandamme's corps, some Sappers and Marines of the Imperial Guard, who had been sent forward to repair the bridge at Charleroi in the event of it having been destroyed, attacked a barricade defended by the enemy, who standing firm however, drove the French Marines back, and according to Vaulabelle, Soult's cavalry division led by Pajol himself, charged the barricade and galloped into Charleroi. It is only right I should add that Thoumas, the cavalry historian, alleges that the bridge was really taken by the Sappers and Marines. There was only one battalion near it, and the men doubtless feared being cut off, if they stood too long. In the meantime General Reille with the 2nd Corps had taken possession of Marchiennes-au-Pont, and the Prussians falling back on the road to Fleurus, the French now held the three bridges of Marchiennes, Charleroi, and Chastelet, on a frontage of 6½ miles.

When the advanced guard of the French left column attacked the Prussian outpost in Thuin, it was driven on Marchiennes, which was defended by a battalion and two guns. The bridge was barricaded and held for some time, the defenders afterwards retiring on Gilly.

At 2 o'clock the 2nd Prussian brigade concentrated near Gilly; thus two brigades retarded the advance for many hours, but this was owing to the absence of infantry at the head of the French columns.

The river Sambre at Charleroi flows at the foot of steep hills over which passes the road to Fleurus. The possession of each separate undulation was vigorously disputed by the Prussians, who were reinforced constantly from the neighbouring cantonments. They were however gradually driven back by the French infantry which was now coming up, but General Zieten, whose advanced posts had been surprised near Thuin, and dispersed, managed to assemble some 8000 infantry, cavalry, and several batteries of artillery, and up to half-past one the French made no further advance. It was then Vandamme passed through Charleroi with orders to move on Gilly and push the enemy beyond Fleurus.

Reille with the 2nd, and D'Erlon with the 1st Corps, were ordered by Napoleon, about 2 o'clock, to advance on the Brussels road, passing through

Gosselies, and drive back any of the enemy's posts they might meet. These orders had just been sent off, when, between 2 and 3 P.M., Marshal Ney appeared. About 3 o'clock in the afternoon the head of Vandamme's 3rd Corps came in front of the position taken up by General Pirch, but the first attack, made in small numbers, made no impression on the Prussian troops.

Napoleon now arrived at Gilly, where he found Marshal Grouchy and General Vandamme halted, for they imagined that there was a large force in their front. The Emperor, having himself reconnoitred, saw that the Prussians were in no great strength, and directed a heavy fire of artillery on their guns, which being silenced the French columns advanced to the attack. General Zieten did not however await the assault, but retreated towards some woods lying to the North-East of the Prussian position. Napoleon, irritated at the thought of the enemy escaping him, ordered his Aide-de-Camp, General Letort, with four squadrons of the Imperial escort, to cut off the retreat of the Prussians, and at the same time Pajol sent forward some of his cavalry to seize a defile in the woods of Fleurus. Letort and the Escort charged home: a battalion formed in square, was broken, losing half its numbers, and another was severely punished, but the rest escaped through the wood with a loss of about two battalions. This success was won however at the cost of Letort's life, for he fell mortally wounded. Meanwhile Exelmans' Dragoons had deployed on the far side of the wood, and successfully charged the enemy retreating across the plain towards Fleurus.

Napoleon left Gilly before the conclusion of the fight, going back to Charleroi to see if all the army had crossed. He now decided that he would divide his troops into two wings, to be commanded by Grouchy and Ney respectively, holding in his own hand the command of the Imperial Guard, Reserve Cavalry, and the 6th Army Corps. As the Emperor rode off, he desired Grouchy to push forward as far as possible towards Sombref, and Pajol and Exelmans continued the advance in that direction. When however Grouchy gave the order to Vandamme to follow the cavalry in support, that General emphatically refused to obey, having received no intimation that he was to pass under Grouchy's command, and he directed his (the 3rd) Corps to bivouac.

Napoleon expected that all his troops would have crossed the Sambre river before noon, but the Staff arrangements were faulty, and at nightfall on the 15th, Lobau's corps (the 6th), half the 4th Corps

(Gérard's), half of the cavalry of the Guard, and two of Grouchy's Reserve cavalry corps were still on the Southern bank of the river.

While Napoleon was overpowering the Prussian rear-guard near Fleurus, Ney was at Frasnes with the 2nd (Reille's) Corps, which he had overtaken at Gosselies some time previously, but on hearing the heavy cannonade at Gilly, the Marshal hesitated to advance further Northward. General Colbert (Edward), who was leading the advanced guard of Reille's Corps with one squadron of Polish Lancers, which had formed part of the Emperor's escort at Elba, charged a battalion of Prince Bernard of Saxe Weimar's brigade to the North of Frasnes, but the battalion standing firm, beat off the squadron. Colbert's regiments, now coming up, moved round to the North of the Nassau battalion, but eventually withdrew to Frasnes about 4 o'clock and reported the occurrence to General Lefèbvre Desnoëttes, but no fresh orders were issued; indeed, Ney had then returned from the vicinity of Frasnes to Gosselies.

If Ney had followed up the Nassau battalion immediately, there is little or no doubt that he might have occupied Quatre Bras without difficulty, but hearing artillery away to the East, the guns being those of Grouchy's Cavalry Corps in action at Gilly, the

Marshal decided to defer its occupation till the morning, and went back himself towards Gosselies, and thence later to Charleroi. Soon afterwards he learnt from cavalry patrols that nothing of importance had occurred at Gilly, and he might even then have resumed his march, but his soldiers, after being seventeen hours under arms, had already bivouaced, and he permitted them to rest. Ney has been blamed for not having executed the Emperor's order on the subject. Vaulabelle says the Marshal sent word to Napoleon that he had occupied Quatre Bras with an advanced guard, but the evidence for this assertion does not appear to me to be conclusive, and according to Soult's statement the Emperor neither gave, nor ever thought of giving, such an order.

Field-Marshal Blücher received at Namur early on the 14th news of the French concentration, and he sent orders for Pirch's and Thielmann's corps to concentrate, and advance. Pirch got to within two hours' march of Ligny by sunset, and Thielmann reached Namur about five hours' march from Ligny, both Corps moving at daybreak on the 15th to support Zieten, who, as we have seen, was falling back from Charleroi. General von Bülow's corps only received its orders on the 15th, for it appears that General von

Gneisenau, who wished to save the feelings of his superior officer, couched the order in somewhat vague terms ; in consequence of these indefinite instructions Bülow did not march till the 16th, and eventually got to Gembloux after nightfall that day, in time, however, to succour the three Prussian corps retreating from Ligny.

An officer despatched by General von Zieten, to announce that his outposts had been attacked near Thuin and were falling back, reached Brussels at 3 P.M on the 15th June. General Baron von Müffling, who received the communication, asked the Duke of Wellington if he would now concentrate, and on what point, stating that Field-Marshal Blücher intended to assemble his army at Ligny. The Duke would not decide immediately, for he had always held that the attack on the capital of Belgium would be made by the Mons road, which was the usual line of traffic, and was ten miles shorter than that by Charleroi. He therefore declined to give any definite orders before he heard news from Mons, where the Allied Light cavalry were watching the frontier. Lord Hill, who was in command at Grammont, heard during the night of the 13-14th June that the French outposts and picquets in his front had all fallen back towards Maubeuge. It is remarkable that his Lordship learnt to within 5000 men the strength of the French force which was then assembling.

The Duke of Wellington, to satisfy Baron von Müffling, promised, on the evening of the 15th, to order a brigade of Light cavalry to march at once to Quatre Bras, and sent out orders for the troops to concentrate at Oudenarde, Grammont, Enghien and Hal, and to be held in readiness to march at a moment's notice. Shortly before midnight the Duke heard from General Dörnberg that the enemy had moved away from Mons, and he went to the celebrated ball given by the Duchess of Richmond, leaving Brussels himself soon after seven A.M. on the 16th. I shall show, further on, the grave risks which were incurred by the delay in sending out the orders. This might have been avoided to some extent if Wellington had proceeded himself on the 14th to Nivelles, about which town the chief portion of the infantry of the 1st (or Left) Army Corps was cantoned. There can be little doubt that the Duke should have done this, and that Picton's (Reserve) division and the Brunswick troops should have been moved up to Genappe earlier.

The cavalry, for convenience of forage supply, had been cantoned by brigades, and in some cases by regiments, on the Dender river. The excuse of the

French advance being unexpected has been alleged as the reason for not having formed the seven brigades into Divisions, but this is inadmissible, and it was the cause of the loss of many lives on the 18th June.

Lord Uxbridge, who was in command of all the cavalry, rode over from Ninove, twenty miles, to Brussels on the afternoon of the 15th, and after conferring with the Duke of Wellington at the Duchess of Richmond's ball, returned to his Headquarters, thence sending out orders for a concentration at Enghien which is twenty-five miles to the Westward of Quatre Bras. Some regiments moved at 6, some at 8 A.M., all the men carrying three days' biscuit. Lord Uxbridge apparently expected the Duke of Wellington would go to Braine le Comte, for he sent Captain Wildman, his Aide-de-camp, to meet him there; but Uxbridge himself rode towards the sound of the guns, and eventually left the field of Quatre Bras about 5 P.M. to hasten the arrival of the cavalry. At Nivelles hay-bags were thrown away and the troops moved at the trot to Quatre Bras, the leading regiment (11th Hussars) arriving only at 8 P.M., too late to take part in the action, and though the brigades had marched from thirty to forty miles, the greater portion of the mounted troops got no further than Braine le Comte that night.

E

E battery, Royal Horse Artillery, marched before daylight on the 16th, moving from Paemale, a village twelve miles West of Brussels, to take post to the North of Ninove, thus heading away from Quatre Bras Later an order was received for it to move through Grammont on Enghien, where it was attached to Vivian's cavalry brigade. It covered, according to Lieutenant Ingilby's diary, some fifty or sixty miles, and bivouaced after dark at Braine le Comte, having only halted once to feed the horses.

* I have not been able to make the march more than fort miles on the map, but both he and an officer of the Royal Dragoons record, that the track followed was very circuitous.

CHAPTER III.

BATTLE OF LIGNY, 16TH JUNE.

Description of country around Fleurus and Ligny.— The undulating plain bordering these villages is broken up abruptly, a mile and a half to the North of Fleurus, by a deep semi-circular ravine which, starting at the Western end of St. Amand, passes by that village and runs up to Ligny, circling round at the foot of a plateau, in the shape of an amphitheatre, on the summit of which stands the hamlet of Bry. Blucher put his army behind the ravine, the two flanks being covered by Ligny and St. Amand, and the front by the little stream which rises near St. Amand. It is only a brook, but the Northern bank, being about two feet higher than that on the South side, increased the difficulty of crossing it. The country to the Southward of these two villages is completely open, giving a good field of fire to the guns of the opposing forces. The front of Blücher's troops massed between Bry and the ravine was covered by many batteries, while the wings, besides resting on St. Amand and Ligny, were further protected by troops in extended order occupying the gardens of the two villages. These enclosures were closely surrounded by fruit trees* which hid the villages ; the church and some of the taller houses only being visible from the brook.

The three Corps present under Blücher were those of Zieten, Pirch, and Thielmann, numbering 97,000 men, of whom 8000 were cavalry, with 220 guns. To oppose this force Napoleon collected about 68,000, of which 13,000 were cavalry. He had 210 guns.

General Count Gérard, whose troops had been standing to arms since daybreak, received only at 9.30 A.M. the order to move forward, and having arrived in front of Ligny, he ordered his men to fall out and rest, while he himself went forward to reconnoitre the enemy's position, accompanied by Staff officers and a few Hussars of the 6th Regiment. When near the Prussian line of front, a body of cavalry advanced against him, and the General and his escort retreated at full speed. During the flight, the General's horse fell in a ditch which was hidden from view by the high standing wheat crops, and the whole of his escort, seeing the General down, turned back to defend him. His Aide-de-camp, Lafontaine, having killed two Prussian Lancers, and broken his sword

* Since cut down.

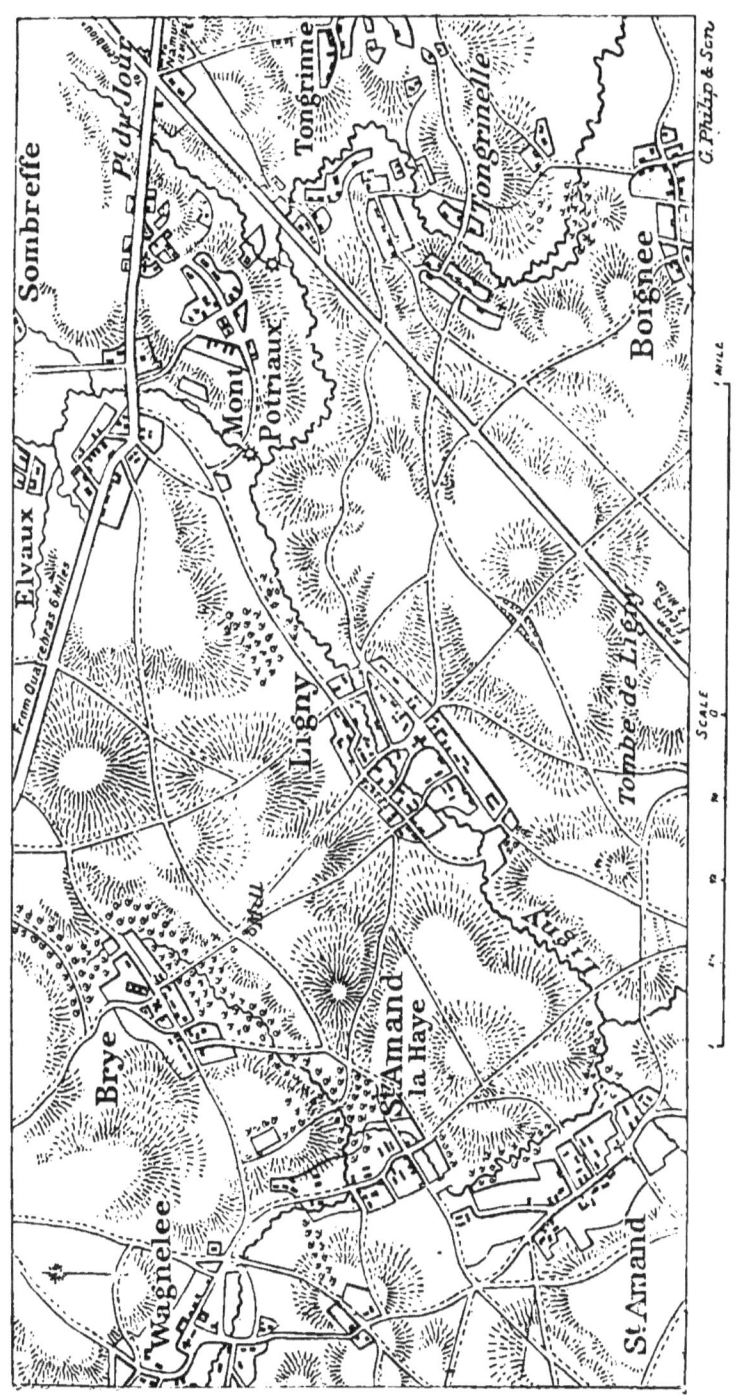

the head of a third, was struck in the side by a bullet fired from a pistol close to his body. The chief of the Staff, Saint-Remy, was dangerously wounded by seven lance thrusts. Another Aide-de-camp, Captain Duperron, dismounted and tried to put Count Gérard up on his horse, but in the hand to hand fighting there being waged this became impossible, and the General must have been killed, or taken, had not a cavalry regiment, led by Grouchy's son, who was attracted by the sound of the firing, galloped up, and driven off the Prussian horsemen.

Soon after 3 P.M. the sound of heavy firing from the direction of Quatre Bras was heard at Ligny, and Napoleon gave the signal for his troops to advance to the attack. For the next five and a half hours a desperate struggle was waged for the villages bordering the ravine. It is not part of my task to enter into details of infantry combats which were not materially affected by the action of horsemen. It may, however, be well to make clear the reason which prevented the use of the Cavalry until twilight, and thus deprive the French of the fruits of their victory, for when the Prussians were driven back in disorder, it was only the falling darkness that saved them.

Count D'Erlon himself thus explains the movement which neutralised his Army Corps: "Between

11 and 12 o'clock, Marshal Ney ordered me to advance on Frasnes and Quatre Bras, where I should receive further instructions, and having told the General who commanded the head of the column to push on, I went forward myself to see how General Reille's corps was getting on. I halted on the North side of Frasnes, where I was joined by General Labédoyère, who showed me a note which he was carrying to Marshal Ney. This note ordered the Marshal to direct my Army Corps on Ligny, and ran thus: 'If you are too closely engaged by the enemy, draw back and content yourself with maintaining your position with Reille's corps, and without losing a minute send word on to us.' General Labédoyère explained to me that he had already given the order to the head of my column to wheel to its right, and pointed out to me how I could best rejoin it.* I turned back, sending my chief Staff officer to Marshal Ney to inform him that I was marching on Ligny."

The 1st Corps got on the wrong road, and instead of marching on Bry as he intended, it moved towards Fleurus.† When D'Erlon saw he was mis-

* This was about 4.30 P.M.
† This false direction added to the uncertainty felt by Vandamme's troops as to the nationality of the Army Corps alluded to further on.

taken he countermarched, and eventually got into position behind Bry so near the Prussians that the men at the head of the column could read distinctly the numbers painted on the backs of the Prussian soldiers knapsacks. D'Erlon's artillery came into action and were just about to open fire when General Delcambre arrived with a positive order from Ney for D'Erlon to bring back his Corps immediately to Quatre Bras. It was then about six o'clock, and D'Erlon was three hours' march from Ney's position. He had to decide whether he should fall on the rear of the Prussians while Napoleon attacked them in front, or carry out Ney's orders. Had he attacked, nothing could have saved the right wing of Blücher's army; but he decided otherwise, and, preceding his men, who were worn out with fatigue, reported himself to Ney at nine o'clock, just as the fight at Quatre Bras ceased.

During the prolonged struggle carried on by Vandamme and Gérard against very superior forces, Napoleon retained the Guard out of action, hoping every minute to hear that Count D'Erlon was falling on the right rear of the Prussians. The French infantry however had reached the North bank of the brook, and were forming on the lower slopes of the Bry position, whence Blücher, coming up, drove the French back over to the South bank of the stream. At five o'clock General Gourgaud, returning from Ligny, where he had been watching the fight, reported to Napoleon that Gérard had engaged the last man of his Reserve. Napoleon then decided to send in the Guard, which moved forward at 5.30. At this moment several officers rode up to announce the appearance of a column of from 25,000 to 30,000 men, marching on Fleurus. It does not seem to have occurred to anyone about Napoleon that this might be D'Erlon's corps, and the suspicion arose, confirmed by the reports of several of Vandamme's officers, that the column was English. One of the divisions (3rd Corps) fell back, and Napoleon was warned that unless Vandamme was supported he must retreat. The Guard was therefore halted to be kept in hand, and several officers of the Staff were sent at a gallop in the direction of the unknown Army Corps. Soon after 6.30 these officers returned, and said that the column had disappeared, and at 7.30 P.M. the Emperor sent forward the infantry of the Guard, and a portion of Milhaud's Cuirassiers. The rest of the Cuirassiers, Horse Grenadiers, and Dragoons received the order to advance by St. Amand and attack the masses of Prussian troops near the windmill on the summit of the Bry hill.

There can be no question of the propriety of D'Erlon's conduct up to the moment of the arrival of

General Delcambre, who ordered him to rejoin Ney at Quatre Bras. Some officers argue that on receipt of this positive order D'Erlon had no alternative but to obey ; but this view is, I think, unsound. The measure of obedience to be exacted from a junior officer, and from one high in command is different. A Commander of an Army Corps should strive to carry out the spirit, and not the literal words only, of an order sent, as in this case, without any knowledge of the situation where the order is received. D'Erlon's men had already made a long march, and as the result shows, it was absolutely impossible for them to rejoin Ney in time to influence the battle, which he was then fighting seven miles to the Westward.

About sunset the cavalry of the Prussian left Army Corps had sustained a serious reverse. Between seven and eight o'clock in the evening, the Chief of the Staff, von Gneisenau, foreseeing the storm about to burst on the centre of the Prussian position, sent to the extreme Left, and desired General von Thielmann to detach two cavalry brigades through Sombref towards Ligny. Shortly before Thielmann received these instructions, he imagined he perceived the French making a retrograde movement, and, in order to harass the retreat, he sent two squadrons, followed up by a battery of Horse artillery, along the high road, directing the remainder of his Reserve cavalry under General von Hobé to follow the battery.

Exelmans was standing on the South side of the brook. He had manœuvred his command very skilfully, holding in check the left of the Prussians, while Pajol watched Boignée further to the Eastward, and Milhaud supported Gérard's right. Exelmans' two divisions had been under fire in an open plain all the afternoon. He had only twelve cannon to reply to over thirty guns, but about five o'clock in the evening he had driven back several battalions which endeavoured to cross the river. At sunset Exelmans saw von Hobé's force coming forward, and according to both the Prussian and French accounts he handled his regiments very well. Placing three guns on the road itself, he opened fire with "case" shot the moment that the head of the Prussian column appeared, his other ten guns coming into action two hundred yards further to the rear, protected by the 5th Regiment of Dragoons, which was skilfully concealed behind an undulation of the ground. The Prussians were caught on the crest of the hill about midway between Mont Potriaux and Tongrinelle, by the 5th Regiment of Dragoons, which, deploying at the trot, broke into a gallop, and, supported by the 13th Dragoons, rode headlong into the enemy's column and overthrew it.

The French took five Prussian guns, which were immediately reversed and directed on the main body of von Hobé's still advancing column. The Prussian general drew the column back, and Exelmans having received positive orders that he was not to follow von Hobé's men, who, although routed, were not scattered, they were pursued by only one squadron commanded by Captain Letellier, who in the excitement of the moment followed up the enemy until he came in front of General von Thielmann's Army Corps, whence he was driven back with a loss of several men.

The Prussians were now however about to experience a greater disaster. When the Imperial Guard was going forward under the eye of the Emperor, the French artillery near Ligny was completely silenced, and soon to those sitting on the Windmill hill it became apparent that the French batteries were moving back. This circumstance misled Field-Marshal von Blücher into imagining the attack on Ligny had been repulsed, and he sent an Aide-de-camp with an order to Röder's Reserve cavalry to take up the pursuit. The Aide-de-camp passed Count Groeben, who was on the borders of the Ligny ravine whence he had observed the approach of Milhaud's Cuirassiers on the East side of Ligny, and he recalled the Aide-de-camp and sent him to General von Röder with an order to bring up three regiments as quickly as possible, to oppose the impending attack of the French Cuirassiers. Colone von Lützow, the celebrated partisan leader, was the first to arrive at the head of the 6th Uhlans, and just at this moment the Field-Marshal also appeared. A few moments later at the North-East corner of Ligny the situation became very grave for the Prussians. There were several French battalions across the ravine close to them, and on the Northern side of the brook seven of the enemy's cavalry regiments were deployed in line. Von Blücher rode forward to the left of the 6th Uhlans, and thus got out of the great crush of the opposing forces close to Ligny.

As the 6th Uhlans were galloping down against the infantry, they came across a hollow way, which, hidden by the corn, was unperceived till too late. It broke up the formation, and during the temporary check caused by this obstacle, the Uhlans were fired into at close quarters, and the Colonel, 11 officers, and some 70 men fell. A second volley completely repulsed the attack, and as the regiment turned, the Cuirassiers followed it up, and von Lützow was captured.

Generals Gneisenau, Grohleman, and the officers of the General Staff were all swept back from Ligny up the hill towards Bry, the enemy making for the windmill as his objective point.

As Blücher was endeavouring to rally his soldiers, his charger, a present from the Prince of Wales, was shot, and began to falter in its stride. Looking at the advancing Cuirassiers, he exclaimed to his Staff officer Nostitz, "Now I am done for!" Presently the gallant horse fell, and rolled on its rider who was ridden over not only by Prussians, but by the French cavalry. As the struggling masses surged backwards and again forwards, the Prussian commander-in-chief was trampled on several times. He lay half-stunned under his horse for nearly a quarter of an hour, but the Aide-de-camp retained his presence of mind, and dismounting, threw a cloak over the Field-Marshal. Then Nostitz, with the help of four Dragoons, pulled away the horse's carcass, and eventually in the darkness got Blücher up on another horse, and led him away from the field of battle.

While Milhaud's Cuirassiers were achieving this success, Exelmans and Pajol passed through Ligny. This village is much more open and spacious than St. Amand, and offered facilities for concentration. From it the Cavalry fell on the flank of the Prussian infantry, which, being attacked at the same moment in front by Gérard's corps, gave way, were sabred and put to flight; and by 9.30 P.M. the Prussians had retired from St. Amand, and resistance ceased in the open country, although Bry, Sombref, and Point du Jour were occupied by rearguards till midnight.

Nobody has criticised more plainly the failure of the Prussian cavalry than German authors. One of the best known writes :—" It is not astonishing that battalions filled with half-trained recruits and others formed entirely of militiamen, should have been unable to cope, when formed in extended order, with the French attacks, directed as they were by Napoleon himself, as the sun went down on the 16th ; but it is more difficult to explain why the Reserve Cavalry was not employed to better advantage. General Jürgass was an experienced leader of Horse. He had held commands in 1813 and 1814, and amongst his five brigade commanders, General Sohr had established a reputation of being a most determined leader of men, and von der Marwitz was also held in high repute."

The same German writer holds that "the true Cavalry instinct was lacking on this occasion: that the five brigades were scattered, and no attempt was made to mass them;" but this I must observe is not quite accurate, since General von Gneisenau, at one time of the battle, collected ten and a half regiments nothing however came of this concentration, and they were apparently again separated before the critical moment.

It was no doubt right to detach Colonel von der Marwitz's brigade to the West to join General Jürgass after D'Erlon's army had been seen advancing in that direction; but no satisfactory explanation has been given of the comparative inactivity of the other brigades. Von Thümen's brigade did nothing near Wagnelée. Von Sohr's brigade, which was between the last-named village and Bry, attacked by single squadrons the French skirmishers as they were coming forward from St. Amand, but without any decisive result; and General von Zieten appears to have considered it was necessary to hold back von Treskow's brigade, in order to ensure the safety of the Prussian batteries on the hill of Bry. We have seen that von Lützow's brigade was checked in its charge by a hollow road, which up to the moment of the attack had not been perceived; but as the Prussian army had been for ten hours in position, it is difficult to explain satisfactorily this ignorance of the ground.

BATTLE OF LIGNY, 16TH JUNE.

The French lost on the 15th and at Ligny 11,000 men, and the Prussians lost 25 guns and 18,000 on the 15th and 16th June, while two days later 10,000 more, enlisted from what had been French provinces, retired to Liège without orders.

Bülow arrived at Gembloux during the night (16th-17th) with 36,000 men, and behind his Army Corps the remnants of Zieten, Pirch, and Thielmann's commands rallied.

CHAPTER IV.

QUATRE BRAS AND GENAPPE.

A TRAVELLER from Charleroi to Brussels, on arriving at the last of the houses dotted about on the heights of Frasnes, sees the high road traversing a vast, undulating, and wooded plain, on which, three miles farther North where the cross-roads meet, stands a cluster of farm buildings. This is Quatre Bras. Between Frasnes and Quatre Bras there are no hedges and there is not a ditch worth mentioning, except in the valley which divided the French and English positions, and in which stands the manor house and farm buildings of Gemioncourt. North of this valley, the only hedges were those bordering the isolated house standing on the East side of the Brussels road, and two hundred and fifty yards South of the farm buildings of Quatre Bras. On the West side of the road was the Bois de Bossu,* which

---

* Cut down by the Duke of Wellington's order when the property was given to him.

To Sart à Avelines
½ mile.   To Namur.

PIERMONT

Pond

Field Track

Gemioncourt

QUATRE-BRAS

& Charleroi

From Frasnes

From Piermont 800yds

WOOD

BOSSU

1 2 3 4 5 6 7 8 880 yards.   1 Mile

running for two thousand yards in a South-Westerly and North-Easterly direction to the Nivelles-Namur road, and closing in gradually on the Charleroi-Brussels road, left only a clear space of about a hundred and fifty yards near Quatre Bras. West of Gemioncourt the Eastern border of the wood was five hundred yards from the high road. In the wood rose a small stream, which, flowing from West to East, passes immediately North of the Gemioncourt farm buildings, and forms a pond half a mile East of the Charleroi road, and a quarter of a mile South of the Nivelles-Namur road, here running in a North-Westerly, and South-Easterly direction. The deepest part of the valley, which is about two hundred yards in breadth, was (and still is) bordered by hedges impassable for mounted troops, and through which infantry could only move in single file. The ground inside the two hedges is from three to five feet lower than that outside, and this added to the difficulty of passing through them.

A mile to the East of Gemioncourt, and a quarter of a mile farther South, is the hamlet of Piermont; and three-quarters of a mile to the West of the high road, and somewhat farther to the South, is the farm of Pierrepont, outside the South-East end of the copse of the same name, which adjoins the Bossu wood

The ground slopes gradually from Frasnes Northwards, to within half a mile of the Gemioncourt stream, and then ascends slightly for a quarter of a mile, forming a ridge, which is well marked, on the West of the road, about five hundred yards South of the stream. Then the ground falls again, rising somewhat abruptly on the North side of the stream. Here the boundary hedge of the valley enclosures is on a low ridge, which is sufficient to afford cover from the higher ground farther South; and then the ground falls a little, rising again with a gentle slope to Quatre Bras.

At the Northern end of this shallow basin, stretching three-quarters of a mile from East to West, and about 500 yards from North to South, stands Quatre Bras, the highest point of the roads which there meet. The scene of the five hours' struggle, measuring from the Southern edge of the Gemioncourt enclosure to the farm buildings at Quatre Bras, is about three-quarters of a mile; and on this limited space and in the wood of Bossu the fight was waged with alternating success. This wood, in some parts close and intricate, was generally passable by cavalry in "extended order," and during the action French batteries had no difficulty in moving inside the enclosure and there coming into action. The fields on which the cavalry charged were covered with wheat and rye-grass, which, generally harvested in July, was as high as the men's shoulders, and concealed in the

WELLINGTON.

undulating ground the movements of even mounted troops.

General de Perponcher, who commanded the

2nd Dutch-Belgian Division, moving from Nivelles, reached Quatre Bras at 3 A.M. on June 16th, and began immediately to recover the ground from which his brigadier's outposts had been driven the previous evening, and by 6 A.M. he had succeeded in re-occupying the Southern end of the Bossu wood, and also the farm of Grand Pierrepont.

The Prince of Orange, who commanded the 1st Army Corps, arrived between 6 and 7 A.M., and occupied the farm of Gemioncourt, two battalions of Dutch militia being advanced immediately South of it; and the prince, endorsing Perponcher's aggressive attitude, sent forward two batteries of artillery up to the ridge South of the Gemioncourt brook.

When Ney was riding round his outpost line to reconnoitre the allies about 10 A.M., the Duke of Wellington arrived at Quatre Bras and at 10.30 A.M. he wrote (in French) to Prince Blücher, as follows :—

ON THE HILLS BEHIND FRASNES
(this was on the ridge South of the Gemioncourt brook).
16th June, 1815.

MY DEAR PRINCE,—My army is situated as follows :—The Prince of Orange's corps has one division here and at Quatre Bras, and the rest of it is at Nivelles. The Reserve is marching from Waterloo on Genappe, where it will arrive at noon. The

English cavalry will be at the same hour at Nivelles. Lord Hill's corps is at Braine le Comte.

I do not see many of the enemy in our front, and I am waiting for news of your Highness, and the arrival of (my?) troops, to decide on my operations for the day. Nothing has been seen of the enemy, either near Binch or on our right.—Your very obedient servant,

WELLINGTON.

The Duke must, almost immediately, have followed the messenger carrying this letter, for after having approved of the positions taken up by the Prince of Orange, he rode out to the Prussian position about seven miles to the Eastward, and meeting Blücher near the windmill of Bussy, just to the Southward of Bry, discussed the situation with him.

It is now well known that Count Gneisenau did not completely trust the Duke, and in spite of all the efforts Baron von Müffling made to impress on him the loyalty of the English Commander-in-Chief, the Prussian Chief of the Staff, who in respect of strategical questions was virtually Commander-in-Chief, placed but a hesitating reliance on anything that the Duke stated.

Blücher, on the contrary, a less able but perfectly straightforward man, believed in Wellington as thoroughly as he did in himself. Von Gneisenau's mistrust was probably partly due to the difficulties of communication, and to the fact that he knew from von Müffling that the Duke's statements, as to the concentration of his army, were inaccurate. We shall see presently that instead of the British cavalry arriving at Nivelles at noon, only the two leading brigades reached that place about seven in the evening. The Artillery and the rest of the Cavalry did not get that night nearer the battlefield than Nivelles. The 11th Hussars got to Quatre Bras at nightfall, and a part of the regiment went at once on outpost duty. The remainder of General Vandeleur's brigade bivouaced near the Bois de Bossu, and the Union brigade, a short distance to the North of Quatre Bras, both brigades linking their horses.

The Duke's dislike of publicity regarding this campaign has caused us to lose many valuable lessons of war. In a letter dated 25th June, 1815, he complains of having "the worst staff ever brought together." It had been forced on him by the Commander-in-Chief, but we cannot learn even now how all this serious miscalculation came to pass, or why some of the Horse Artillery (Webber-Smith's troop), which was at Alost, thirty-five miles distant, did not reach Quatre Bras till 10 A.M. on the 17th June.

During the discussion which ensued at Bussy mill von Gneisenau urged that the Duke of Wellington should, after concentrating his force, march towards

Bry to support the right rear of the Prussian army. The effect of this movement would have been to leave open the Charleroi-Brussels road; yet however much the Duke may have disliked the plan, he

SIR THOMAS PICTON.

observed as he rode away:—"Well, I will come provided I am not attacked myself." Soon after 2.30 P.M., when the Duke returned to Quatre Bras, the Prince of Orange's advanced troops were being driven back, and his Artillery had retired on either side of the Gemioncourt enclosure, with a loss of two guns.

QUATRE BRAS.

Sir Thomas Picton arrived at Brussels from England during the night 15-16th June, and his division, with the Hanoverian Militia of the 6th division, had left Brussels at 5 A.M., carrying three days' biscuit and some meat, and after halting in the forest of Soignies for two hours to cook the dinners—which were, however, thrown away in obedience to orders before they were ready—came into position at Quatre Bras between 3 and 3.30 P.M. The 3rd Division came up soon after five o'clock, and the Guards arrived only at 6.30 P.M., thus the brunt of the fight fell on de Perponcher's, the Duke of Brunswick's, and Picton's troops.

It was 2 P.M. before Ney was ready to move forward, and his artillery opened fire. He had then 1700 cavalry, 16,000 infantry and 38 guns, while the British force numbered but 7000 infantry with 16 guns. The audacity shown by Perponcher and the Prince of Orange, and a want of enterprise in reconnoitring on the part of the French cavalry, caused Ney to imagine that the Allies were in much greater strength than was the case. He could from the high ground near Frasnes count his opponents standing between Gemioncourt and the Nivelles-Namur road, but could not tell what troops were on the reverse slope

North of that road, or behind the Bossu wood though either of Piré's brigades, which were a Frasnes over-night, might have obtained this information, and with impunity, by riding round the British flank. Piré, however, did nothing to ascertain this all-important fact; and Ney, with a personal knowledge of Wellington's skill in concealing troops in defensive positions in Spain, would not advance until Foy's division arrived at Frasnes, about 2 P.M. At 2.15 Bachelu moved East of the high road, extending his right flank to Piermont, the advance being covered by the 1st Chasseurs (Hubert's brigade) of Piré's division. The other brigade (Wathier's) and 6th Chasseurs (Hubert's) moved in the centre, and immediately charging rode over one of the battalions of Dutch Militia, South of Gemioncourt, before it could form square. It rallied, however, in the farm buildings.

About 3 P.M., as Picton's division approached Quatre Bras, Bachelu's infantry seized Piermont, and he massed several battalions to assault Gemioncourt, which was still held by the 5th Regiment of Dutch Militia. General de Perponcher, and the Prince of Orange, now placing themselves at the head of another battalion of this regiment, marched down the high road to support those in front. The supporting battalion came under a heavy fire from the French guns on the ridge South of Gemioncourt, and not being sufficiently trained to fight in extended order, eventually had to fall back, as did also the battalions from the Manor house. Just as Picton's division got into position on the Nivelles-Namur road, Jerome's division attacked Pierrepont farm, and the Southern edge of the Bossu wood. The 95th (British) Regiment was hurried down to try and save Piermont, while the 28th was sent forward to occupy Gemioncourt; but both these places were strongly occupied by the French before the British battalions approached. As the Dutch fell back from Gemioncourt, von Merlen's Light brigade of Dutch-Belgian cavalry advanced to cover the retreat. The 6th Chasseurs approached with the points of their swords lowered, shouting to the Belgians to rejoin the army they had but recently left. They refused however; but, on being vigorously charged, fled up to the cross-roads, where they rallied on the Northern side of Quatre Bras, the French drawing rein on seeing British infantry; about this time the Dutch-Belgian infantry, abandoning four guns to the enemy, fell back into the Bossu wood.

Up to 3.30 P.M. the strength of the French infantry was unchanged, but Guiton's brigade of Cuirassiers, 800 sabres, had arrived; the Allies now had 18,000 infantry, and 2000 cavalry (Continental), which were thus placed :—

Perponcher's men held the Bossu wood to within a hundred yards of the stream ; the Duke of Brunswick who, bringing 3000 infantry and 1000 horse, had arrived soon after Picton, was in the open on the West of the road parallel to the front of the Dutch, and about 600 yards South of Quatre Bras, near which stood the 92nd (Highland) Regiment (Pack's brigade). Immediately South of the Namur road, and East of the Charleroi-Brussels, road was Picton's division, Pack being on the right, Kempt on the left ; and in support stood Best's Hanoverian Militia brigade. The wood lying between Quatre Bras and Sart à Avelines, the Southern end of which extended down to the Namur road, a mile to the South-East of Quatre Bras, was defended then, and throughout the day, against the French, by the 95th Regiment (Kempt's brigade) in spite of many efforts to take it.

Ney's extreme left held the Bossu wood up to the stream, his centre was firmly established at Gemioncourt, and his right at Piermont. He had massed his guns on the ridge to the South of Gemioncourt, whence they nearly silenced the Allied artillery, and played with great effect on the infantry as it came into position, the Duke of Brunswick's men being within

700 yards and Picton's troops at from 1000 to 1200 yards range.* The Duke of Brunswick's raw troops were severely tried by the casualties which they suffered in rapid succession, but were well commanded by the Duke, who personally showed the greatest courage.

Ney presently sent forward two heavy columns into the valley East of Gemioncourt ; and Wellington, fearing for the safety of the Brunswick troops, ordered Picton, about 4 P.M., to leave the 92nd at Quatre Bras and advance. Both British brigades moved forward in line, East of the Charleroi road. The collision with Kempt's brigade occurred on the Northern slope of the ridge North of the Gemioncourt valley, the French not perceiving their foes, who were concealed by high rye-grass, until the British regiments opened fire. The heads of the French column, as the opponents closed together, were outflanked, the men hesitated, fell into disorder, and at Picton's command the British, cheering, charged, bayoneted, and routed the French columns, driving them through the hedgerows into the valley. On the extreme British left, the 79th Regiment crossed the valley (two hundred yards

* These distances are taken from the batteries on the West side of the high road, the battery to the Eastward being 200 yards farther back.

in breadth) and pursued up to the main French
position, from whence, however, it was driven back by
two battalions of the 108th Regiment, which had been
kept in hand ready to support the French attack
The British battalions re-formed on the ridge North
of the valley, the Northern hedge being held by the
English, while the French rallied behind the Southern
boundary fence. On the right of the line the 42nd
and 44th Regiments, crossing the hollow, nearly
got possession of the Gemioncourt Manor house and
out-buildings; but these, being strongly held, could
not be secured, and the two battalions falling back
re-formed in line with Kempt's brigade.

Just as this occurred, Foy's division advanced from
the stream, one brigade on the Brussels road, the
other between it, and the Bossu wood. Behind the
skirmishers marched a battalion in line, supported by
two columns, and Hubert's cavalry brigade, which
was now concentrated, while Wathier's brigade began
to advance on the Charleroi road from near Frasnes.

The Duke of Brunswick, finding that he had not
room for two cavalry regiments between the high
road and the wood, sent the Hussars back to Quatre
Bras, while he himself, at the head of the Lancers,
charged the enemy's advancing infantry. The French
battalion, forming rapidly from line into square,

easily repulsed the Lancers, who galloped back to Quatre Bras, and the leading French squadrons following boldly, the Brunswick troops broke and fled. While the Duke was trying to rally his infantry, he was mortally wounded, a little to the East of the garden of the isolated house which stands two hundred and fifty yards to the South of Quatre Bras. The Brunswick Lancers, pursued by the Chasseurs, galloped in a crowd on to the 92nd, then lining the shallow ditch of the Namur road close to Quatre Bras. The Highlanders wheeled back one company, let the horsemen through, and then fired with great effect into the leading French squadron, the men of which, with those immediately following, were thrown temporarily into confusion; but the main body of the Chasseurs soon re-formed, and retired in good order.

The Brunswick Hussar regiment was now ordered forward from Quatre Bras, to attack the 6th Chasseurs; but being fired on by the French infantry advancing on the Eastern skirts of the wood, the Hussars hesitated and then turned from before their opponents, who pursued so closely that the whole were mistaken by our men for Allied cavalry retiring. The Chasseurs following the Hussars got through the 92nd men, behind whom the Duke of Wellington

G

took refuge, escaping from his pursuers only by jumping the little fence of a garden which was lined by a company of the battalion. The Chasseurs continued to cut down fugitives and stragglers in Quatre Bras, until, seeing that they were isolated, they tried to retire by breaking through the 92nd from the rear. Few of these brave Frenchmen eventually escaped. An officer who, coming from the rear, personally attacked the Duke of Wellington was shot through both legs by some soldiers who faced round just in time, and his horse fell dead as he reached the Duke.

Wathier's Lancer brigade (5th and 6th Regiments) did not follow up the Chasseurs, but having passed the right flank of the two foremost British regiments 42nd and 44th, wheeled round and attacked them in their rear. The 42nd was in the act of forming square, and all but the two rear companies had run in, when the leading squadron of Lancers overtook them, and, spearing many, broke into the square. Nevertheless the other faces were steady, and gradually closing inwards, these bayoneted all the French men who had followed the rear company. The, however, died hard, killing the commanding office, and the two next senior officers; the command thu changing hands four times in a few minutes' struggle

The 44th, standing on the left (Eastward flank) of the 42nd, had not time to alter its formation, the thud of galloping horses' hoofs being the first indication of the coming storm. Colonel Hamerton, facing both ranks about, reserved his fire until the Lancers were close up, when a volley destroyed many of the foremost. With undaunted courage, however, individual men pressed on; and one grey-haired old Lancer, riding straight at the colour party of the 44th, severely wounded Ensign Christie, who carried one of the colours, driving the lance through his left eye to the lower jaw. The Lancer then endeavoured to seize the colour, but Christie, with marvellous endurance and determination, dashing the flag to the ground, threw himself on it. The Frenchman succeeded in tearing off a portion with his lance, but was eventually bayoneted by the nearest soldiers, and thus the colour was saved. The Lancers, repulsed from the rear of the 44th, galloped away to the Eastward, and having got round the proper left flank of the battalion, moved by its front to the Westward to regain the bridge on the main road, suffering severely from a volley poured in from the left company of the line, which had reserved its fire till now.

During this first attack made by Wathier's brigade of Piré's division, the commanding officer of the 28th Regiment, Colonel Belton, arrived from England, and assumed the command; and about forty-eight hours afterwards he received the command of the brigade, when Pack took over Picton's division on the death of that officer.

Piré's shattered cavalry Division recrossed the Gemioncourt brook; and thus ended, shortly before 5 P.M., the first main attack. Ney had driven the Dutch-Belgians and Brunswick troops to the North of Quatre Bras, and his artillery had severely punished Picton's division. Pack's brigade, on which the Lancers had fallen, lost during the day's fighting 800 out of 2200 men, and the two right-hand battalions, 42nd and 44th, were so much reduced that they reformed in one square. Towards the conclusion of this struggle, Ney's infantry got possession of the Bossu wood nearly up to its Northern end, and he had advanced two batteries inside the wood close to its Eastern boundary. From the wood he sent two columns against the isolated house. The leading battalion seized the building, and when its supporting column came out of the wood, moved forward to Quatre Bras. It was now, however, charged vigorously and pushed back by the 92nd Regiment, and though the supporting column attempted to hold the house and its enclosure, whence the men fired with grea

We will now turn to the movements on the French side.

Kellerman, setting out from Charleroi, had trotted, without drawing rein, twelve miles to Frasnes, where he arrived at 2.30 P.M., with his leading division, and from that time it had remained dismounted. The other division was ordered by Ney to remain at Liberchies, half a mile South of Frasnes. At 6 o'clock Ney sent an order to Kellerman to bring up one brigade, but no orders were sent at the moment to the other three brigades of the Cavalry Corps which were within reach, nor to the Light Cavalry of the Guard, 2100 strong, under Lefèbvre Desnoëttes, whom Napoleon had placed at Ney's disposal. As Kellerman approached, Ney galloped up, and excitedly shaking him by the hand, repeated, perhaps unconsciously, the text of a letter which he had just received from Napoleon. He said: "My dear General, a great effort is necessary; on you perhaps depends the fate of France; you must charge, and break through the infantry in our front. Advance, and I will have you supported by all Piré's cavalry." As Kellerman, with Guiton's brigade of the 8th and 11th Cuirassiers, each 400 strong, trotted down the Charleroi-Brussels road, along which he rode in order to cross the

Gemioncourt brook, the following was the position of the English troops:—

The square formed by the 42nd and 44th, which stood on the low ridge overlooking Gemioncourt, was suffering from the fire of the French artillery and skirmishers, who were pressing across the valley from the Gemioncourt farm buildings. The three battalions directly under Halkett's command were "preparing for cavalry," on the West side of the road. As the 69th, warned by the Aide-de-camp, was in the act of forming square the Prince of Orange, who commanded the 1st Army Corps, rode up, and in a loud voice asked what the battalion was doing? The Commanding officer explained that he had been ordered to form square, as the enemy's cavalry was advancing; but the Prince ordered him to get into line, saying he did not believe in an attack being imminent; yet 800 sabres were at this moment crossing the brook within 400 yards! As Kellerman's men passed over it the Head of the column was wheeled to the left, and the regiments formed in lines of columns in succession as the Rear cleared the bridge. There is a hollow at this spot, which, in conjunction with crops five feet high, must have completely hidden the brigade.

In front of the 8th Cuirassiers rode Kellerman, and Brigadier-general Guiton. They passed behind the right flank of the 42nd-44th square, and, with the right squadron on the road, came opposite to the 69th, whose men saw nothing until Kellerman, perceiving that the Infantry was unprepared, wheeled the leading squadron of Cuirassiers by sections to its right, when within a hundred yards of the right flank of the line, and, dashing on, completely rolled up the battalion. In less than two minutes 150 of the 580 men of the 69th were lying on the ground dead or dying, and those uninjured were dispersed in every direction. Some officers and men took shelter under the bayonets of the 42nd-44th square; the mounted officers fled by the West of the road back to Quatre Bras, pursued by a troop of Cuirassiers, and then only escaped by riding through one of the Hanoverian battalions on the Namur road. Major Lindsay, Lieutenant Pigot, and Mr. Clarke, a volunteer, resisted desperately. The last-named officer killed three Cuirassiers, and although himself wounded in twenty-two places by sabre cuts, preserved the colour he was carrying. The other colour, taken by Cuirassier Henry, was sent back immediately South of the brook, and paraded along the front of Foy's infantry, just before it started to support the cavalry attack, the trophy being greeted by the French soldiers with enthusiastic cheers. The remainder of the 8th Cuirassiers passed on towards Quatre Bras, and now the 11th, moving on the West of the road, was approaching Halkett's other battalions.

The 30th Regiment, which had also deployed by order of the Prince of Orange, saw Kellerman's advance in sufficient time, and, getting hastily into square, awaited the attack, although on two sides the men stood six instead of four deep. The 11th Cuirassiers charged simultaneously two faces of the square; but the infantry, standing firm, beat off the leading squadrons, which Kellerman himself rallying, led towards the right of Halkett's brigade. Avoiding the 73rd (British) and two Brunswick battalions, which appeared to be steady, the Cuirassiers advanced against Halkett's right battalion. It had been in square on the rising ground close to Quatre Bras, where it had been fired into so heavily by the French batteries from within the wood, at case-shot distance, that it had become necessary to deploy into line, and in that formation the battalion was advancing as the Cuirassiers approached. It had, however, become unsteady after the fall of its senior officers, and breaking up ere Kellerman closed with it took refuge inside the wood.

Up to this moment Kellerman's attack had achieved considerable success. He had ridden óver two battalions, and his regiments had kept the remainder of the infantry in squares, which formation had offered an easy target for the French artillery. The Cuirassiers now, however, suffered severely, not only from the fire of the battalions which stood grouped around them, but also from British artillery which had just come into action on the Namur road.

While these attacks were being executed by Guiton's regiments, Wathier's Lancer brigade (Piré's division) had advanced to the East of the road, and made several gallant but fruitless attacks on the squares standing firm in that part of the field. On more than one occasion, where the tall rye-grass hid the battalions from the view of these daring horsemen, individual Lancers, riding up to within fifty yards of the British squares, stuck their lances in the ground as a point for the squadron officers to lead on. Several squadrons of Cuirassiers and of Wathier's Lancers attacked vigorously and simultaneously three sides of the square formed by the (28th) Gloucestershire Regiment. The men, however, steadied and encouraged by General Picton shouting their historic battle cry "28th remember

Egypt,"* remained firm, and reserving their fire till the horsemen came within fifteen paces of the bayonets, then with deadly volleys repulsed the foe.

Near the Namur road, the 6th Lancers under command of Colonel Galbois, who two hours earlier during the first charge, had distinguished himself by his audacious leading on the 42nd Highlanders, attacked a Hanoverian square, which they rode over and dispersed. Being however surrounded by other battalions, the Lancers suffered heavy loss, but carried off their Colonel, who had been dangerously wounded close under the serried bayonets he had tried to break through.

Kellerman, having, as described above, routed two British battalions, collected his men, and attempted to advance up the Brussels road. As they moved on, they passed under a heavy fire from two guns at case-shot range. From the houses of Quatre Bras also, and from the North-East corner of the Bossu wood, there came a shower of bullets: and presently Keller man's horse fell dead on its rider. Up to this time

* On March 21st, 1801, the 28th, when hotly engaged with an enemy in its front, was attacked in rear by a column, which, concealed by the mist, had got round the battalion. The rear rank was faced about, and the simultaneous front and rear attacks were repulsed. The regiment still wears a head-dress with numbers both in front and in rear, in commemoration of its brave conduct on this occasion.

between 6.30 and 7 P.M., the Cuirassiers, inspired by the leader whom all knew by sight, or by repute, had shown courage seldom surpassed ; but when Kellerman fell, they fled, deaf to the commands and entreaties of their officers. Galloping over everything in their path, they carried Wathier's brigade away with them in a tumultuous mob. Kellerman, though much shaken, was not seriously hurt, and supporting himself on the necks of two of his men's horses, he ran out of action. As Guiton's Cuirassiers with Wathier's Lancers galloped wildly to the rear, they took with them the Chasseur brigade which had not been closely engaged in the last attack. Two miles from the field the flying mass came on 2500 cavalry, and these men, although dismounted, were drawn into the stampede. The crowd of fugitives did not indeed stop until it got past the hospitals on the South side of Frasnes, and up to where the cavalry of the Guard stood. Foy's infantry columns, which had gone forward after cheering Kellerman's initial success in overthrowing the 69th Regiment, became demoralised at the sight of the flying horsemen, and began to give way, and but for Ney would have followed the retreating cavalry. The hero of Redinha (Spain), and of many rear-guard fights in Russia (1812), dismounted, and with great personal exertion restored order.

By nightfall the French were driven back to the position they had held in the morning, the English holding Gemioncourt and the Southern end of the Bossu wood.

The respective losses of the Allied troops indicate by which nationalities the brunt of the fighting was borne :—

The British lost	2,200
The Brunswickers	800
The Hanoverians	360
The Dutch-Belgians	(doubtful)

The French lost about 5000 men.

OBSERVATIONS.

It is remarkable that although Ney had an explicit order to unite the 2nd Corps (Reille) and Kellerman's Cavalry Corps, yet he failed to employ more than one brigade of the four under Kellerman. Mr. Ropes, who, in his 'Campaign of Waterloo,' has devoted immense care to sifting all the available evidence on disputed points of the four days fighting, argues, and as I think soundly, that Ney thought it was unwise to operate decisively with the Left Wing of the Army so far in advance of Napoleon who was still before Ligny. Ney had also at his disposal Lefèbvre Desnoëttes' Light Cavalry of the Guard, but I should mention that he had been warned it should be spared as much as possible.

I have animadverted, in the narrative, on the want of enterprise shown by Piré's cavalry division in not venturing to pass round the West side of the Bossu wood. There would have been no difficulty in reconnoitring round this flank, nor on the Eastern flank through Piermont, and up the Namur-Nivelles road. Information of De Perponcher's weakness would have been of great importance to Ney, for, had he known there was but a handful of men in his front, he could easily have seized Quatre Bras before that place was reinforced.

Piré's first attack was well designed, the movement of the supporting brigade of Lancers in reversing their front and attacking the rear of Pack's brigade being in itself a bold conception. In the execution, however, there was a want of combination; the leading squadrons and individual men charged with devoted courage, but these attacks were disunited: and the squadrons in front opened out to either flank and retired, while those following generally did the same, but without closing on the bayonets. If at the moment that the leading squadron rode into the rear of the 42nd square, the side faces had been also attacked, the battalion must have been overwhelmed.

A perusal of French accounts of Quatre Bras shows most English versions of Kellerman's charges to be inaccurate. Even the Standard authority makes the Cuirassiers take part in the attacks which were finished by 5 P.M. Now, Kellerman's men did not advance from Frasnes till after 6 P.M., and his report (of which, by the courtesy of the late French Minister of War, Général du Miribel, I hold a copy), dated at 10 P.M. June 16th, shows clearly that he took part only in the last attack. His success was obtained, to quote from his report, over " an indomitable infantry, whose cool courage enabled them to fire as if on a drill parade." Marmont puts Kellerman as the first of the only three French cavalry leaders whom twenty years of war produced. His prompt change of front, when he saw over the top of the rye-grass the open flank of the 69th Regiment, showed that the hero of Marengo had lost nothing of the quick decision which enabled him, fifteen years previously, with 400 sorely tried cavalry, exhausted by eight hours' fighting, to overthrow 2000 victorious Austrian Grenadiers. It was, however, a mistake on his part and that of his Brigadier-general to ride together with the leading squadrons in the attack ; moreover, and possibly in consequence, the supporting regiment, 11th Cuirassiers, entirely failed to make any impression on the

30th and 73rd British regiments, not having been led straight on the squares with the determination which characterised the attack of the 8th Cuirassiers.

The Rank and File were animated by personal devotion to the Emperor, but their mistrust of officers for the greater part personally unknown to them is comprehensible, seeing that many of these had gone from the Napoleonic Government to the Legitimists, and back again within twelve months. The want of confidence in squadron leaders, obtained only by long association, is plainly shown from the panic with which the cavalry were stricken after Kellerman fell. We learn also another lesson from this afternoon's work, for although the 6th Lancers, led by Colonel Galbois, probably owing to his personal influence and great courage, achieved a startling success over the Hanoverian battalion near the Namur Road, yet the lessened vigour generally of the second attack is one more proof of the adage that cavalry should not be asked to undertake desperate attacks twice during the same day. It is right I should mention that the Hanoverian battalions had only been recently raised, though they had been trained for two months under British officers.*

In considering how much of the success actually

* *Quarterly Review*, 1815.

attained would be possible over Infantry armed wi[th] the magazine rifle, we must bear in mind that t[he] attacking squadrons were hidden by the tall cro[p] until they got close to the battalions. Magazin[e] rifles would not have helped the 69th Regiment, [as] the men could not see the 8th Cuirassiers until t[he] leading squadron was within a hundred yards of t[he] right flank of the battalion; but on the other han[d] the Cavalry which was beaten off by the 42nd an[d] 44th Regiments, would certainly not have come in[to] action again on the same day, had those galla[nt] battalions been armed with modern weapons.

The actual charges were not, however, the on[ly] service rendered by the French squadrons at Quat[re] Bras. Their threatening attitude kept the British i[n]fantry continually in close formations, in which the[y] suffered terrible losses from artillery fire; and su[ch] was the moral effect produced by these attacks, th[at] many of our battalions slept in square during t[he] night, being apprehensive of a renewed advance [by] the dreaded horsemen.

The British cavalry arrived shortly before nightfa[ll] and bivouaced in fields of standing wheat and barle[y,] the leading brigade on the battlefield and the [re]mainder at Nivelles, and many horses died from havi[ng] eaten the indigestible green crops. During the nig[ht] fine rain fell, adding to the discomfort of the numberless wounded men who were scattered all over the ground between the Gemioncourt stream and Quatre Bras. No further movement was made by the troops on either side until about an hour before daylight on the 17th, when a British cavalry patrol, getting accidentally between the French and English picquets near Piermont, caused a scare which was transmitted all along the line, and was stopped only by the efforts of the senior officers in the French and English armies.

At daybreak on the 17th neither Ney nor Wellington knew the result of the fighting at Ligny. The Duke sent a Staff officer with an escort down the Namur road; and the officer following the line of retreat, learnt at 7.30 A.M., at Tilly, seven miles East of Quatre Bras, from General Zieten, commanding the rear-guard, that the Prussians had retreated, and also that the French had not followed them across the Namur road. Wellington, on receipt of this information, made his dispositions to retire on Waterloo, and about 10 A.M. the cavalry took over the advanced posts, the infantry moving back without molestation into the position in which they fought on the 18th.

At 8 A.M. Count Flahaut, the Emperor's Aide-de-

Camp, who had ridden with Ney all the previous afternoon, returned to Headquarters, and reported the result of the action at Quatre Bras, stating also that the Marshal did not know what had occurred at Ligny. At 9 o'clock Napoleon left Fleurus in a carriage to drive round the battlefield, but he soon had to mount his horse, for it was impossible for the carriage to cross the ground covered with bodies, and which was, moreover, cut up by shallow ditches. The Emperor had intended to march and follow up Wellington early on the morning of the 17th, but was dissuaded by his Generals, who urged that the English were fresh, and their men were tired. On the other hand, the French soldiers grumbled at being held back inactive. It is possibly correct, as Vaulabelle asserts, that misfortune had rendered Napoleon less resolute than he was in his early wars. In previous campaigns he would not have asked the opinions of his Generals, and possibly there was some truth in the remark of the blunt outspoken Vandamme: "Ah! this is not the Napoleon of former days!" We ought, however, to bear in mind, that from 3.30 A.M. on the 12th June, when he left Paris for the frontier, he had been constantly travelling fighting till 11 P.M. on the 16th, when he left the battlefield of Ligny to go back to Fleurus.

At 10 A.M. the Emperor ordered Lobau (6th Corps

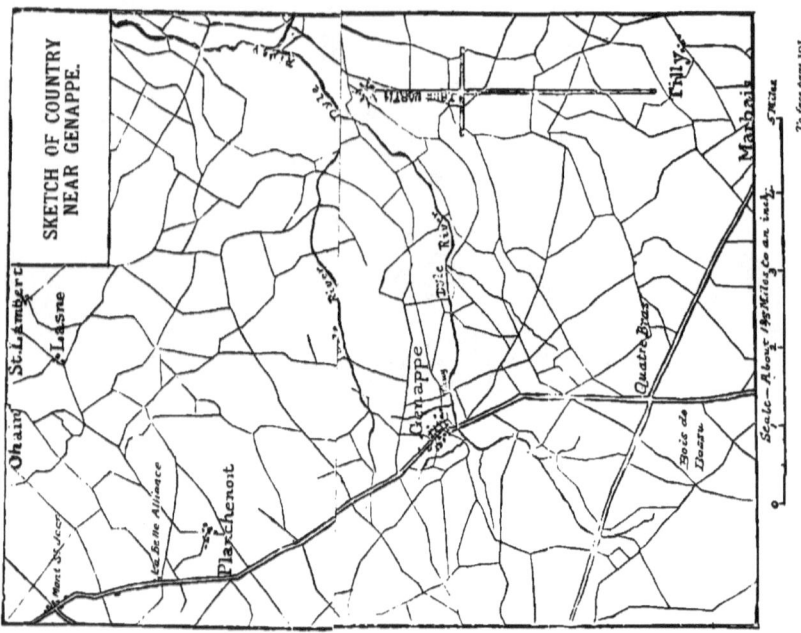

and at 11 A.M. the Guard and Milhaud's Cuirassiers, to march on Marbais, awaiting himself news from Pajol. The French Cavalry had not ascertained the Prussian line of retreat, for though Pajol reconnoitred towards Namur at daylight, no one was sent at first Northward, and it was noon before Napoleon heard that 20,000 Prussians had been seen near Gembloux.

At 12 o'clock, when Grouchy received the order to pursue Blücher, the soldiers, who had breakfasted at daylight, and had been "standing to arms" since the early morning, were cleaning their muskets; a part of the cavalry had "off saddled" to ease their horses, and thus more time was wasted, before the Army Corps went forward; the march also was greatly delayed by the heavy rain which fell from 2 o'clock, and the head of Grouchy's columns did not arrive at Gembloux till 4 o'clock in the afternoon. It was dark when the last detachment reached that village, where Grouchy halted his troops, having covered only six miles.

When about midday Napoleon heard that the English were still at Quatre Bras, he sent orders to Ney to occupy that position. The Duke of Wellington had, however, fallen back before the French reached the cross-roads.

The British infantry retired between 10 and 11 A.M., and the cavalry between 1 and 2 P.M. in three columns, the centre one on Genappe, a well-built town of about 1200 inhabitants. The flank columns were led so as to pass the Dyle river above, and below the town. The left column, composed of Vandeleur's and Vivian's brigades, when crossing by the bridge at Thuy, was followed closely by the French; but the movement being skilfully effected, the troops got across the Dyle before the French had an opportunity of charging, and a squadron of the 10th Hussars dismounting behind a bank, prevented any serious pursuit on that flank.

The morning had been oppressively hot, without a breath of air, the sky being covered by dense, low-lying clouds. When the British guns on the right, or Western flank, opened fire against the advancing French columns, the concussion brought down the clouds, and the noise of the guns was followed by a terrible burst of thunder, accompanied by rain of tropical violence. In a few minutes all movements faster than a walk, except on the road, became impossible, for the horses sank deep in the soft fields, on the high ground up to their knees, and on the lower slopes up to the girths.

Some good work was done by a squadron of the 7th Hussars, left behind on the South side of the Dyle to cover the movement of the Household brigade through the long and narrow stone-paved street of

Genappe, which constitutes a defile for a thousand yards. Lieutenant O'Grady with half of the rear squadron, was posted on the Quatre Bras-Genappe road, when the leading French troops threatened to cut off the remainder of the squadron, then extended in skirmishing order to the Westward. O'Grady, by a succession of bold advances up the road, impressed the French with the idea that they were about to be attacked, and they drew back sufficiently far to enable him to pass the whole of the skirmishers from the flank into the town, whence he regained the North side of Genappe without the loss of a single man. The French then, following up, placed under the personal direction of the Emperor a battery on the right bank of the Dyle, which fired with effect upon the 7th Hussars, then standing on the road at the Northern suburb of the town.

The English centre cavalry column at this time was thus placed :—

Lord Edward Somerset's (1st) brigade and the Horse Artillery were on, or close to, the road, 700 yards to the North of Genappe ; the Union brigade was deployed alongside the 1st brigade in the fields on the West of the road ; the 7th Hussars were on the road itself, with another Light cavalry regiment in support. The paved roadway, standing about one and a half feet above the fields, has here a wide unmetalled track on either side, and three vehicles can move abreast on the causeway without difficulty. It will allow of from twelve to fourteen horsemen moving in line on it, but is bounded on either side by ditches which were then full of water.

As the head of the French column, composed of the P^{lers} (Polish) Lancers in red jackets, appeared in the exit from the street, the front squadron, 7th Hussars, working under the immediate eye of their Honorary colonel, Lord Uxbridge, was let go, and it galloped boldly at the foe drawn up on the road. The squadron was in high spirits, for the rear troop (O'Grady's) had just retired successfully before twenty-four squadrons, and Lord Uxbridge had warmly praised it before the Regiment. The Lancers, putting the flank men close to the walls of the houses, dropped their lance points, and, at the halt, awaited the attack. This was vigorously pushed home, but the Hussars were unable to penetrate the line of steel points. Both the French and English squadron leaders, hemmed in by the crossed weapons, were either killed or mortally wounded,* the Hussars

---

* Major Hodge was mortally wounded and taken prisoner with Captain Elphinstone, to whom the Emperor spoke very graciously for a time, ordering that he should be well treated. Two of the subalterns captured were stripped of valuables and pelisses, but later, during the Life Guards' attack, they caught loose horses and escaped.

failing to break through the Lancers, who were supported by a mass of cavalry massed as thick as the horses could stand. The 7th men fought desperately for some time, but, outnumbered and fired on by French artillery, were eventually driven back. The Lancers now followed them up, when the engaged squadron of the 7th, rallying on its support, drove the Lancers back to the town. Again and again these charges were renewed: as Lord Uxbridge wrote, "a determined see-saw being kept up for a considerable time." The Adjutant was killed. Captains Elphinstone and Peters, Lieutenants Wildman, Grenfell, and Gordon lost their horses, and were taken prisoners; two, however, catching riderless horses escaped during the charge which I am about to describe.

Lord Uxbridge eventually withdrew the 7th Hussars, and, riding to the supporting Light Dragoon regiment,* ordered it to advance. Our men had learnt to appreciate the power of the lance, and Lord Uxbridge's "address not being received with all the enthusiasm he had anticipated,"† he ordered the regiment to clear off the roadway, calling up two squadrons of the 1st Life Guards, under Major Kelly. The Life Guards were at the moment moving in "threes"‡

---

* Page 103.
† *Vide* statement quoted in Siborne's 'Waterloo Letters.'
‡ On a front of six men.

towards Brussels, and "going about," galloped down the roadway at speed towards the Lancers, who at the same moment were advancing at the "trot" up the road, the rising slope of which is about equal to that from Grosvenor Place towards Hyde Park Corner. The Lancers hesitated, went "about" just as the Life Guards reached them, and were overthrown, with considerable slaughter. Colonel Sir John Elley, who was on the Staff, but who had joined in the charge, cut down a Lancer on either side of him as the Life Guards collided with the mass of Frenchmen, and the road and adjoining fields were strewn with men and horses. The whole column, turning in the narrow street, was pursued and driven out of the Southern end of the town.

This was a gallant feat, but the result was never for a moment doubtful. The Lancers were small men on light horses, and could, as I showed in the first chapter, have had but very elementary training. They were trotting up hill as the Life Guards approached. Our big men, on powerful horses, had the advantage of the downward slope, and were animated, as every unprejudiced person will admit, with a greater desire to close with the foe than were the raw troops towards whom they were riding. The French officers, as at Quatre Bras, endeavoured to make up for the want of efficiency in their men by freely hazarding their lives. Lieutenant - Colonel Sourd was badly wounded, his sword-arm being so hacked by sabres as to be practically severed. He had the arm amputated, and, according to Prince Edouard de la Tour d'Auvergne, remounted immediately after the operation, and within an hour was again at the head of his regiment.

The Life Guards, after chasing the French right through the town, withdrew slowly to Waterloo, and the Light Dragoon regiment took up the duties of rear-guard. Between 6 and 7 P.M. Napoleon deployed a division of Heavy cavalry near "La Belle Alliance," and opened fire from four batteries. The Allies replied with sixty cannon, and the French moved back to their bivouacs.

As the evening of the 17th closed in, picquets were thrown out by the French and English outposts, and these movements gave rise to two determined charges made by half-squadrons, one of which, under Captain Heyliger, 7th Hussars, was checked by the Duke of Wellington himself, who, however, commended the gallantry shown by the officer and his troop. In the other charge, half a squadron of the 2nd Light Dragoons of the King's German Legion, advancing from Hougomont up to the farm Mon Plaisir, drove back some French squadrons, and recaptured three carriages laden with British sick and wounded men. As the opposing lines of vedettes, sentries, and picquets got into position, and the artillery on either side ceased fire, a heavy thunderstorm broke, and the rain fell in torrents, to the great discomfort of both forces, which, separated by a distance of from a half to three-quarters of a mile only, were without tents, or any means of shelter. The Allies had the great advantage of having got into position in sufficient time to collect fuel, and soon large fires blazed along the whole of their position. The horses were short of food, but not the men, as is generally supposed to have been the case, for, even allowing for the one day's rations which had been thrown away half-cooked when the troops were hurrying up to Quatre Bras, they should have been in possession of biscuit for the 17th. The soldiers on both sides were wet to the skin. Our men had no great-coats, they having been sent to Ostend, under the idea that they were too heavy to be carried, but the men were all in good spirits when, on passing the grog cask, each received a small tot of gin.

On the French side, however, matters were different. It was 11 P.M. before Donzelot's infantry passed through Genappe, the single street of which was so choked with artillery and baggage waggons that the infantry were obliged to cross the Dyle at Thuy, and thence march across standing crops of wheat and hemp, which wetted their clothes up to the waist, and occasionally in low ground they sank in up to the knee. The night was so dark that they had to move on connecting files of cavalry soldiers placed at two hundred yards distance apart, and who kept on shouting " This way, this way ! " Erckmann Chatrian describes vividly how, long past midnight, companies of exhausted and ravenous men, to satisfy the cravings of hunger, "broke their ranks" in order to dig up radishes and other vegetables in the gardens of the farms they passed, for the provision waggons were far behind, and even on the 18th, when these arrived at 8 A.M., they contained nothing but spirit rations, which were issued without anything for the men to eat.

There was little or no fuel available for the French, and moreover, for some unknown reason, orders had been given prohibiting fires being lighted. Between 2 and 3 A.M. on the 18th the rain lightened a little. Nevertheless day dawned on thousands of men whose clothes were wet through ; but while the French were hungry and cheerless, the large fires kept up by the Allies enabled their men to dry their clothes, and they all had some food.

CHAPTER V.

WATERLOO, 18TH JUNE.

DURING the night (17th–18th) rain fell continually, and sometimes in torrents. Both armies bivouaced in fields of standing crops which were saturated with moisture. The surface of the ground where columns of troops had passed over it was churned up into thick mud, and water stood in all hollow places. When day broke on the 18th, there was no sign of life in the Allied position save among the picquets and their sentries; but behind the centre of the French position Reille's corps was seen coming up from Genappe, beyond which it had not been able to advance overnight. The sky at first was hidden by heavy clouds, but the weather began to clear soon after 9 o'clock, and the sun showed a little after the battle began, although it was never seen in its splendour till just as it was setting, about the time of the victorious advance of the British troops.

The result of the nine hours' struggle was materially influenced by the character and capacity of the leaders on either side; and we may arrive at a better understanding of how these qualities became of value in the battle if we consider briefly the previous history of those who led the cavalry, omitting from our consideration the characteristics of other generals commanding, who, however distinguished previously, were not so prominently engaged.

Major-General Sir Colquhoun Grant joined the 36th Regiment as an ensign in 1793, exchanging (some years later) to cavalry, with which he served at Seringapatam, but returning to infantry in 1802 to command the 72nd regiment, which he led for six years. He exchanged to the 15th Hussars in 1808, and took part in Sir John Moore's expedition, being wounded at Sahagun. He returned to Spain in January 1813, commanding a brigade till the end of the campaign. At Waterloo his brigade was stationed in the centre of the position, and he had five horses shot under him.

Major-General Sir Hussey Vivian, who conducted the last charge made on June 18th, entered the service in 1793 as an ensign in the 20th Foot. After serving in the Low Countries, he exchanged to the 7th Light Dragoons in 1798. He served with Sir John Moore in Spain, later commanding a cavalry brigade—1812-14. He lost the use of one arm in an action which ensued on the armies advancing on Toulouse, after the battle of Orthes.

Major-General Sir John Vandeleur joined the 5th Foot in 1781, and, after becoming a captain in 1792, was transferred to the 8th Light Dragoons, to the command of which he succeeded in 1798. As a colonel he commanded a brigade of cavalry in India in 1803-5, where he distinguished himself greatly on one occasion, taking two thousand prisoners by a flank charge. In the Peninsula he commanded a brigade in the Light (Infantry) Division. Towards the end of that war he was transferred to the command of a cavalry brigade, and held a similar position at Waterloo.

Major-General Sir William Ponsonby, K.C.B., served in various infantry corps until appointed a major in the Irish Fencibles, 1794. Having joined the 5th Dragoon Guards in the same rank, and becoming lieutenant-colonel in 1803, he commanded the regiment 1811-12, and led it at Salamanca (1812), until he succeeded to the command of the brigade after the fall of General Le Marchant in the historic charge which gained that brilliant victory.

Lord E. Somerset joined as a cornet in the 10th Light Dragoons in 1793, and became a captain in

1794. After serving as a major in the 12th Light Dragoons, he commanded the 5th Regiment of Foot. The following year he exchanged to the 4th Dragoons, and with them served throughout the Peninsula in seven great battles, including Salamanca, where his regiment, with two others, took two thousand prisoners. He commanded the 1st Brigade at Waterloo.

Lord Uxbridge was born in 1768, and, like many other of the cavalry generals of whom I am writing, he first entered the infantry branch of the Service, receiving a commission as lieutenant in the 7th Foot in March, 1793. He became a captain in the 23rd Foot the same month, a major two months later in the 65th Foot, and a lieutenant-colonel in the 16th Light Dragoons in June, 1794; in the previous month he had attained the rank of full colonel, thus passing through all the intermediate grades from lieutenant in fifteen months. This is his official or gazetted rank; but it appears that at the age of twenty-five, before he entered the Army, he commanded a battalion which had been raised on his father's estates in Staffordshire on the outbreak of the French Revolutionary war. In April, 1797, his connection with the 80th Regiment, or Staffordshire Volunteers, ceased, on his being transferred to be lieutenant-colonel of the 7th Light Dragoons. In the meantime, however, his Lordship

I

had served in Flanders, and being the senior Field officer in Lord Cathcart's brigade, commanded the brigade during his general's employment in charge of a separate corps. In the retreat from Egmont-op-Zee with one squadron he successfully charged and overthrew six squadrons of the enemy. He rejoined the 7th Hussars in May, 1801, being specially selected by George III., and, as Lord Paget, distinguished himself under Sir John Moore in 1808-9; when Napoleon crossed the Sambre in 1815, he was in command of the seven cavalry brigades then spread out along the line of the Dender river.

If we turn to the French, we realise at once—as did Napoleon, though too late—how much they suffered from the want of able cavalry leaders. There were many brave men under Napoleon at Waterloo; and, as shown in Chapter I., all the generals serving under him were in the prime of life. Napoleon himself was only forty-six years of age, as were Soult, Ney, Lobau, and Kellerman, while all the other generals of note were younger. Nevertheless, the Emperor's brother-in-law, Murat, who would have been the most valuable cavalry leader of all, was absent, and Napoleon bitterly regretted later that he had decided not to employ him. As he wrote at St. Helena, "he would perhaps have achieved the victory for us, for it wanted but little to break three or four English squares." Murat had the great characteristics of inspiring his followers with the utmost devotion, and his enemies with terror. Ney, who led the cavalry as well as the infantry charges on June 18th, however brave, however experienced in war, was, as regards cavalry, but a poor substitute for Murat, and, as will be seen in my story, would not listen to Kellerman, who was far superior to him as a leader of Horse.

Ney had originally served for a short time in the cavalry, but, either because he knew the men and horses were not sufficiently trained to be employed in line formations, or because he personally preferred to use masses similar to those in which he sent forward the infantry, throughout the battle he sent his cavalry forward in successive lines of columns. Thus every horse and rider struck down in the crowded rank entailed the fall of many others.

The question of Napoleon's capacity in this campaign has been recently and fully discussed * by Field-Marshal Viscount Wolseley, and therefore, though the Emperor's health materially affected the use of his cavalry, I content myself with an extract from Henry Houssaye's "1815," the most reliable of all the French authors I have read on "The Hundred Days." In

* 'The Decline and Fall of Napoleon.'

this book there is a striking description of the Emperor's personal appearance by an Englishman

NAPOLEON.

who stood near the Saluting-point at a grand review in the spring of 1815.

"His face is very pale, with pendulous cheeks. I

is not very stout, but the abdomen protrudes so much as to cause his shirtfront to ruck up above the waistcoat." Henry Houssaye pictures, in graphic language, the great change which came over Napoleon between his arrival in Paris the third week in March, after a triumphal progress from the gulf of St. Juan, and his departure for Belgium, three months later. To " Energy, Determination, and Confidence," had succeeded " Languor, Indecision, and Despondency."

No smaller man could have confronted, with a tenth part of Napoleon's success, his overwhelming task. He had to face the most powerful Coalition ever arrayed against a single nation. The North-West and South of France were either in a state of insurrection, or conspiring to rise. After fifteen hours of daily work in reorganising the defences of the country, he was called out to discuss political questions with Constitution makers. There is a remarkable memorandum extant, written to Marshal Davoust, at the War Office, as the Emperor left one of the useless Councils, in which he mentions he had just noticed a regiment marching to the Front without a second pair of shoes, and begs this may be prevented in future. The mental strain was, however, too great for his body, and produced paroxysms of strangury, and induced other ailments.

I need not allude further to the subject of the

Emperor's mental and bodily vigour except to remark that it is impossible to pass by without reference the extraordinary apathy on the part of the French on the morning of June 17th. The Prussians had disappeared from before Napoleon at Ligny. He had within eight miles of Quatre Bras, the 6th Corps, which had not fired a shot, the Guard, which had done no hard fighting, and Cavalry which had suffered but little. It is true the 1st Corps (D'Erlon's) had been marching to and fro all day on the 16th, but it had not come into action, while within two miles of Quatre Bras Kellerman had three brigades of cavalry which had not drawn swords the previous day. While Napoleon was chatting at Ligny, Ney, irritated by the Emperor's interference with D'Erlon's Corps, was sulking at Frasnes, and he made no move till nearly one o'clock, when he saw Napoleon's columns marching by the Namur-Nivelles road on Quatre Bras.

It appears that Soult had taken no adequate steps to find out what had gone on in front of Ney, who had made no report of his previous day's fight, and when Napoleon got to Quatre Bras, he himself realised for the first time what a chance he had missed of attacking the British troops as they fell back. Once he began the pursuit, he showed the greatest activity, personally directing a battery on our cavalry engaged at Genappe.

Henry Houssaye, whom I have before quoted, shows clearly how much Napoleon in previous campaigns was indebted to the businesslike capacities of Berthier, who had just committed suicide. He was not himself a great man, but his methodical nature, knowledge of detail, and perfect acquaintance with Napoleon's habits of thought enabled him to unravel " the most complicated orders, expanding them in every detail with correctness, precision, and admirable clearness." * Soult was very inferior to Berthier as a Chief of the Staff to Napoleon, although a much greater general. It is possible that his being unpopular with officers, rendered the transmission of orders more difficult than usual, and it is never an easy task.

THE BATTLE.

The British cavalry brigades moved about 10 A.M. from their uncomfortable bivouacs, which were knee deep in mud, the horses having trampled the crops under foot, and most of the riders had slept at the horses' heads with an arm passed through the reins, though in some Regiments they were "linked."† The

* 'Revue des Deux Mondes,' p. 796, December 1894.
† Horses are said to be linked when the collar chains or head-ropes are passed through the links of the head-collars of the horses on either side.

brigades of which I am now about to write took up the following positions :—

Somerset's Heavy brigade :—
- 1st Life Guards (2 squadrons).
- 2nd Life Guards (2 squadrons).
- Royal Horse Guards (3 squadrons).
- King's Dragoon Guards, (3 squadrons).

In what we should now term "Brigade Mass," immediately West of the Genappe-Brussels road, and a quarter of a mile behind the crest of the English position.

Total paper strength 1220 sabres.

Ponsonby's Union brigade :—
- Royal Dragoons (3 squadrons).
- Scots Greys (3 squadrons).
- Inniskilling Dragoons (3 squadrons).

East of the road and in line with Somerset's brigade.

Total paper strength 1150 sabres. Officers who were present say about 900 effectives.

Vandeleur's Light brigade :—
- 11th Light Dragoons (3 squadrons).
- 12th Light Dragoons (3 squadrons).
- 16th Light Dragoons (3 squadrons).

In columns, North of the Braine-l'Alleud-Ohain road, and East of the Papelotte-Verd-Cocu road which just there runs in a hollow.

Total 1000 sabres.

Vivian's Hussar brigade :—
- 10th Hussars.
- 18th Hussars.
- 1st Hussars of the German Legion.

In line to the East of the Smohain-Verd-Cocu road with outposts toward Wavre.

Total paper strength about 1200 sabres.

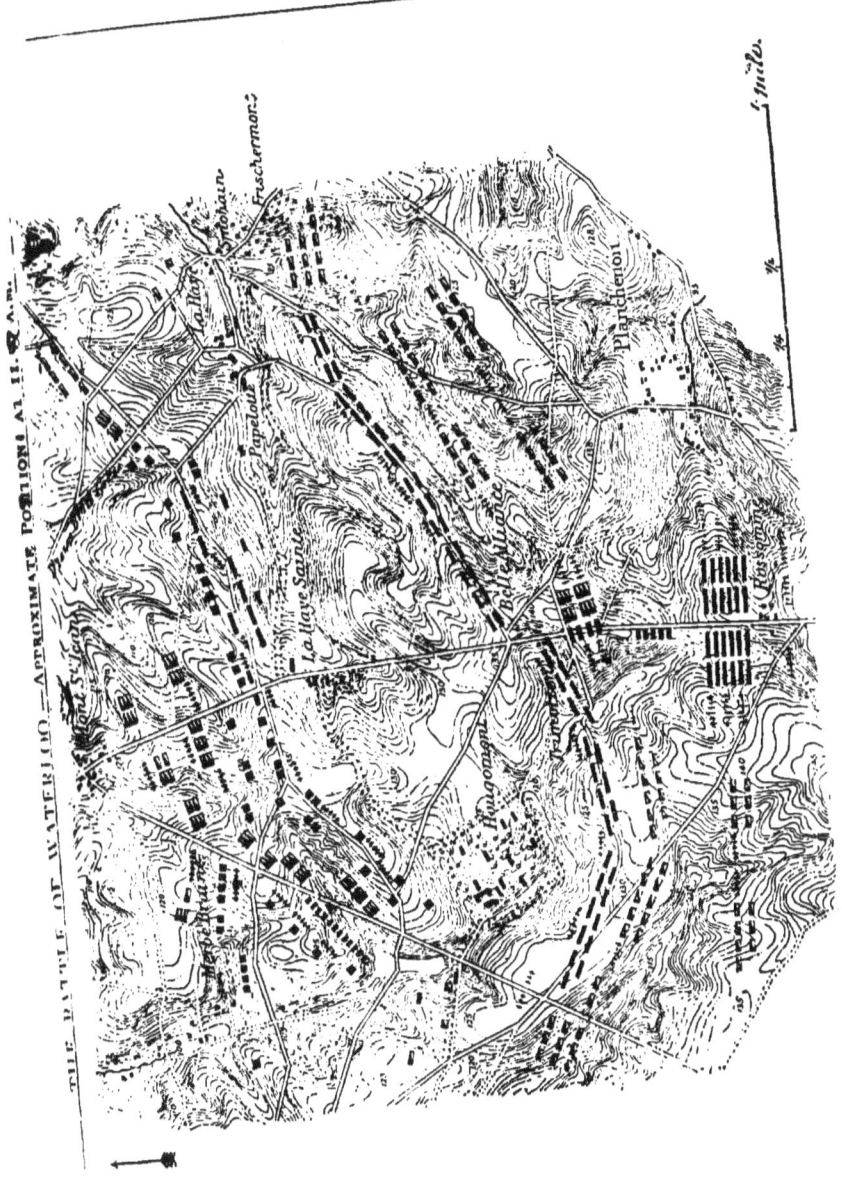

Description of the British Position.

A traveller from Genappe to Brussels, arriving on the height on which stands "La Belle Alliance" public-house, sees the ground falling away in front and, about two thousand yards to the North, a ridge about a mile and three-quarters in length, which is divided into two nearly equal parts by the Genappe-Brussels high road. Along this ridge, on a narrow plateau, was the British position. The crest line runs on the West side of the Genappe-Brussels road, about three hundred yards to the North of the Hougomont enclosure, where the ground falls away sharply; and on the East side it passes five hundred yards to the North of Papelotte, where the ridge merges into the plain. A hollow road, which leads from Braine l'Alleud on the West, by Ohain, to Wavre on the East, and following generally the crest, marked the main line of resistance. This crossway cuts at right angles the Genappe-Brussels high road two hundred and fifty yards North of the substantially built farm of La Haie Sainte. About a quarter of a mile to the West of this farm the hollow road trended out to the Southward; and, as the Eastern portion of the position receded Northwards, the line presented the appearance, from "La Belle Alliance," of being straight in its central portion, with the left flank somewhat drawn back, and the right thrown forward.

The hollow road was bordered on either side by hedges of box and beech; these formed the only fences on the field of battle, and gave the name to the adjoining farm, La Haie Sainte. In 1815,* in some places the roadway ran eight or ten feet below the surface, as was the case immediately to the North of La Haie Sainte, where it constituted a formidable obstacle. On the West of the Genappe-Brussels high road, the average depth of the crossway was six feet.

To the East of the Genappe-Brussels road, the Southern slope of the ridge held by the Allies—*i.e.*, that towards the French—was sufficiently steep to check horses and to render it difficult for men to march in the sodden state of the ground. On the West side of the high road, except just midway between La Haie Sainte and Hougomont, the last ascent to the crest must have been made with difficulty, as the ground everywhere else rose so rapidly that the helmets of the French cavalry, halted a hundred and fifty yards South of the crest-line, were only just visible to our infantry standing on the summit; and

---

* It has been entirely altered in appearance by the removal of an enormous amount of earth for the mound on which the Belgic Lion stands.

our guns, when a little drawn back, were unable to *lay on* troops who were attacking the farm buildings of La Haie Sainte. These stand in a hollow on the West of the road some two hundred and fifty yards in front of the main position. Visitors to the battlefield will be puzzled by all accounts of the battle, unless they recall continually that the mass of earth on which the Belgic Lion stands was built up by cutting away the abrupt rise of ground and sloping it gradually from North to South. The original slope of the ground will be understood by looking at the sections of the contoured plan, page 121.

On the Right flank of the Allied line was Hougomont, a solidly-built structure. The old manor house was surrounded by orchards, which were bounded by high walls, giving great facilities for defence, although these might have been knocked down if they had been open to direct fire; but they were almost covered by a wood which extended nearly a quarter of a mile South of the house and farm buildings. The two farms, Hougomont and La Haie Sainte, being stoutly held as outlying posts, materially affected the result of the battle.

The ridge selected was well situated for a defensive action, as the Northern or Reverse slope gave good protection from view, and some from fire, for while the

Allied cavalry sat on their horses behind the ridge their lances and head-dress only could be seen from the French position. From the crest of the British position every attack, and indeed every movement made by the French, could be clearly foreseen by the Duke, because Napoleon's army being ranged on a ridge which was dominated by higher ground further to the Southward, it was impossible for him to conceal his troops when moving to make either a flank or front attack. To add to the Emperor's difficulties the heavy rain, which had fallen for twenty hours, had made the ground so deep that the guns, when off the ridge, sank up to the axles.

Napoleon spent most of the day, that is from 11 A.M. till 3 P.M., on the so-called "heights of Rossomme"— a long undulating plateau over which the Genappe-Brussels road passes. On a hillock West of the road he sat at a table with a map spread out before him. The ground falls rapidly to the Northward underneath where the Emperor sat, but on the East of the Brussels road the slopes are less steep. The front French line was ranged on the descending slope, nearly parallel, and opposite to the Allied troops, and at an average distance of fifteen hundred yards.

The Allied forces, before the arrival of the Prussians, consisted in all of 68,000 men with 156 guns; while the French numbered 66,000, and 242 guns. The British cavalry, with which alone I am dealing, numbered 7000 sabres. In this calculation the English and King's German Legion only are reckoned, as the Continental cavalry did nothing towards gaining the victory. The French had about 11,100 cavalry actually on the ground. In this estimate I have deducted from the strength known to have been present at roll-call on the 14th, 10 per cent. of Piré's regiments and 15 per cent. of Dubois Cuirassier brigade which had been engaged at Quatre Bras: and 200 of Milhaud's Cuirassiers who fell on the 16th at Ligny. British officers who were present give about 900 sabres as actually representing the number given in the official statement as 1150, in one of our brigades.

It may enable my readers to understand more easily the part the Cavalry took in the battle if we consider the attacks of the French army as divided into five different phases, according to the plan adopted by Colonel Sir Shaw Kennedy, and followed by Mr. Dorsey Gardner.

Authors differ as to the hour at which the battle began, but of this there is no longer any doubt, as we know that General Lord Hill timed the first shot by his stopwatch as having been fired at 11.50 A.M.

Attacks.

1. Reille's corps at 11.50 A.M. attacked Hougomont, around which fighting continued till the sun went down, and although the French persisted with great determination, they were invariably repulsed with loss.

2. D'Erlon's corps attacked, shortly before 2 o'clock, the Allied left and centre, being driven back behind its original position in about an hour's time.

3. The French cavalry attacked the Allied centre at intervals from 4 to 6 o'clock.

4. Ney's attack on the Allied centre began about 6 P.M., and continued till nearly 7.30 P.M.

5. The advance of the Imperial Guards began at 7.30 P.M., the struggle ending after dark with the total rout of the French troops to the South of "La Belle Alliance."

In the second phase, with which my story of this battle begins, Napoleon, after cannonading parts of the Allied position for some time with 120 guns, and sending Light troops against the enclosures South of La Haie Sainte, on which, however, no effective artillery fire was apparently brought to bear, about 1.30 P.M., ordered D'Erlon to advance; and his Corps of four Divisions, numbering 16,000 men, moved forward in direct echelon from the Left, at four hundred paces interval, under the protection of the fire of a line of batteries, in all 74 guns, which were established on the crest of the central *under feature*, 250 yards South of La Haie Sainte, and about 600 yards from the crest of the English position.

These four Divisions consisted of eight brigades. Each had four battalions, except Donzelot's division, which had nine. Each battalion was deployed in line at five paces distance (giving only sufficient room for the officers) between the battalions.

As Donzelot and Marcognet's divisions moved forward, their rear brigades were each re-formed into "demi-brigades" (*i.e.* two battalions), which moved in support of the leading brigades. D'Erlon's attack stretched from Papelotte on the East to La Haie Sainte on the West, and was supported by Bachelu's division of Reille's Corps, and Roussel's cavalry division of Kellerman's command. The flank brigades of the Corps were the first to come into collision with the Allies. The farmhouse of Papelotte, held by a single company, was captured immediately, but was soon retaken; and I need scarcely again refer to this, the extreme Eastern flank of the battlefield.

In advance of the general line of the Allied

position, Bylandt's Dutch-Belgian brigade stood on the slope in front of Picton's division, which was not visible from the ridge occupied by the French.

The farm of La Haie ·Sainte with the orchard to the Southward of the buildings was held by Baring's battalion of the German Legion, and on the open sloping ground to the West of the enclosures some companies of the same battalion were extended. As these were driven back by the French skirmishers who were leading the left echelon of D'Erlon's attack, the Duke of Wellington, who was at the moment on the crest immediately above the threatened point, sent down the Lüneburg battalion from Kielmansegge's brigade. Baring seeing the reinforcements coming down, went forward to recover the orchard which the French had seized, and was already driving back the enemy, when he saw a Cuirassier regiment approaching. It had advanced when the German skirmishers were seen to be retiring.

As the Horsemen drew near, the skirmishers ran towards the orchard, and colliding with the (Lüneburg) battalion, threw it into disorder, and the Cuirassiers, coming boldly on, rode down and sabred all those who were outside the enclosures. The Cuirassiers re-formed under the crest of the British position, immediately below where Kielmansegge's

K

and Ompteda's brigades stood in square. While thi[s] was occurring, Lord Uxbridge was preparing [a] counter stroke not only to D'Erlon's attack, but als[o] to the charge of the Cuirassiers, who, emboldened b[y] their success in riding down the Lüneburg battalio[n] were now coming on to assail the main position.

There are serious discrepancies in most of th[e] Histories as to the exact time, but it was probabl[y] shortly before 2 P.M. when Lord Uxbridge, who ha[d] been to the Cavalry brigade on the extreme Righ[t] on returning to the centre of the position saw th[e] Lüneburg battalion being sabred below him, and th[e] French columns advancing against Picton's divisio[n]. His lordship galloping up to the Union brigad[e] ordered it to form line, and advance to within [a] hundred yards of the crest, where it was to wait an[d] conform to the movements of the Household brigad[e]. No orders, nor even an intimation of this intende[d] attack was sent to the next brigade, but Sir Joh[n] Vandeleur, writing in October (?) 1836, mentions th[at] he had before the battle received instructions t[o] engage the enemy when he thought proper witho[ut] waiting for orders. Nevertheless I shall show furth[er] on, that this freedom of action was not well establishe[d] in his mind at the time the aid of his brigade w[as] most required, nor indeed was such a lease of Ind[e-] pendence intended by the Duke of Wellington to be given to any Brigadier.

As D'Erlon's four columns, covered by skirmishers, passed through the great battery of seventy-four pieces, the guns ceased to fire, reopening again with good effect on Picton's division, and with still more deadly results on Bylandt's Dutch-Belgian brigade, which was well down the Southern slope of the ridge, as soon as the rear of the French columns had descended the hill sufficiently far to allow of the projectiles passing over them.

When the closely-packed masses reached the low ground in the valley, the tall standing crops and saturated soil rendered it difficult to maintain regular formation in the ranks. There was, moreover, according to French accounts, something weird in the appearance of the British position; for, except Picton's skirmishers and Bylandt's brigade, no infantry could be seen, and the guns appeared to be entirely unsupported.

The rear brigade of the left division (Quiot's*) attacked La Haie Sainte, and the leading (Bourgeois') brigade, which was advancing parallel with the high road, inclined away from the farm and the sand pit

* Its commander, General Allix, was absent on special duty.

near the cross roads, on being punished by heavy fire poured in on the mass from Kempt's brigade. It thus crowded the division (Donzelot's) immediately on its right, and came with it, up to the left front of Kempt's brigade, from the unseen fire of which both Divisions now suffered terribly. Nevertheless the surging columns, covered by skirmishers, moved on, and with drums beating, and men shouting "Vive l'Empereur," got close up to the road, where Bourgeois presently attempted to deploy. Some French writers state that the columns were now already so unsteady as to be foredoomed to fail.

Just before this time, however, Picton had advanced his division; Kempt was moving forward in line; and Pack also, but somewhat in his left rear. Picton had only the remnants of two brigades, about 3000 men in all, for he had borne the weight of the French attacks on June 16th, at Quatre Bras; and now some 10,000* of the enemy were marching through a gap into his position, for Bylandt's Dutch-Belgian brigade after losing many men from the French artillery fire had retired in disorder before the coming storm, and could not be rallied till its battalions reached the extreme rear of the British position.

As the French columns, having ascended the hill

* D'Erlon's rear division (right rear) numbering 4,000 men was not yet up, and one brigade was assailing La Haie Sainte.

approached the hedge which bordered the hollow road, they suffered heavily, for immediately North of it were British batteries which poured forth case shot up to the moment of the enemy reaching them. The French guns had now again ceased to fire, and there were renewed shouts of "Vive l'Empereur." Just as the British skirmishers ran in, Kempt, with whom Picton rode, brought his brigade up to the hollow road, and at the same moment the French, who were within fifty yards of it, on receiving a hot fire, endeavoured to deploy. It was at this moment that Picton ordered the charge to be sounded. The front rank of Bourgeois' column fired ; and as Picton fell, shot through the head, it seemed as if the thin British line, disordered by passing through the sunken road, and hedges, was about to be overwhelmed, not, however, by the column in its front, but by the massed battalions then surmounting the ridge farther Eastward.

Siborne, the Standard British historian, but one who wrote mainly from an infantry point of view, implies that Kempt's brigade had defeated Bourgeois' column before it felt, on its flank, the effect of the cavalry charges which I am about to describe ; and Sir James Kempt asserted that he "had completely effected the repulse of the enemy when the Union brigade charged" another column. On the other hand, Captain Seymour, the Aide-de-camp referred to below, says the Highlanders were overpowered when Picton called to him to look to them. The English line was firing, and there were tall crops in front and around the combatants, thus there is ample scope for difference of opinion, but it seems certain that the collision of the "Royals" with the enemy was on the crest of the position and Bourgeois' brigade could not therefore have been previously repulsed. Our gunners apparently thought the situation was critical, because one gun was so securely spiked that it remained out of action all day!! Whatever may have been the actual facts, and there was glory enough for all *Arms*, Picton's last words to the Aide-de-camp —" Rally the Highlanders" (of Kempt's brigade), and Pack's appeal to a battalion—"92nd, you must charge: all in front have given way!"* are not indicative of victory ; but less importance would be attached to these points if Picton's division had possessed any Reserve, but there was none. There can, I think, be no doubt that a part of Donzelot's division, which cleared Kempt's left flank, and the leading column of Marcognet's division, had both reached the crest of the British position when Somerset's and Ponsonby's brigades charged, and the attack

* This evidently was not meant to apply to Kempt's brigade, but to Bylandt's.

of the British cavalry was, in any case, the cause of the overwhelming disaster to D'Erlon's corps.

Let us deal first with the Household brigade, with which Lord Uxbridge rode forward, almost immediately after he gave the order to attack. The 1st Life Guards, and two squadrons King's Dragoon Guards on the right of the line, met Dubois' Cuirassiers at the foot of the steep slope immediately North and West of La Haie Sainte, the enclosures of which divided the Household brigade as it rode forward. These separated also Dubois' brigade.

The 1st Life Guards and the French Cuirassiers collided, as an eye-witness declares, "like two walls," but the result was never for a moment doubtful. The Cuirassiers had already been engaged, and although they had achieved a brilliant success in cutting up the Lüneburg battalion, were naturally not as steady as before that combat. The British troopers were far better trained, were mounted on much bigger horses, and with all the advantage of the descending slope, had passed over just enough distance to obtain momentum without their horses being exhausted. After the collision the Cuirassiers turned, and many tried to escape by galloping down the Genappe-Brussels road. The 2nd Life Guards and the left squadron King's Dragoon Guards now struck into Dubois' right Regiment. As it advanced, it crossed the Genappe-

Brussels road at the cutting, from which the squadrons were emerging in some confusion as our men galloped at them.* Organised resistance was hopeless under these circumstances, and the Cuirassiers fled, while the 2nd Life Guards, bringing up their right shoulders, crossed the road, and eventually became mingled with the Union brigade, to which I will now pass.

In consequence of Bylandt's brigade having retired from the front, there was a considerable interval between Kempt's and Sir Denis Pack's brigade, for Picton had not sufficient men for the ground allotted to his division. Kempt's regiments stood from right to left in the following order: 1st Royals, 42nd, 92nd, 44th —the latter being somewhat in rear of the left of Best's brigade.

When Lord Uxbridge personally warned Sir William Ponsonby that he was to be ready to attack, conforming to the Household brigade, that General having advanced his brigade a short distance, halted it in order to keep the men under shelter until the opportune moment for charging should arrive; but he rode forward himself to the crest of the ridge, accompanied by Colonel Muter, commanding the

* It was in this cutting Trooper Shaw had his first personal encounter. A Cuirassier awaited him at the halt and tried to run him through. Shaw parried the thrust and clove the Frenchman's brass helmet and head in twain.

Inniskilling Dragoons. Sir William was riding an unsteady horse, and had dismounted to readjust his cloak on the saddle, when the near approach of the French column, and the movement of the Household brigade showed that the moment for action had come, and he told his Aide-de-camp, De Lacy Evans, to give the prearranged signal by holding up his hat. Simultaneously the 92nd advanced by order of Sir Denis Pack. Some few minutes previously the Scots Greys, to avoid loss from artillery fire, had been moved a short distance to the left rear. At this moment, however, the officer commanding the regiment saw the head of Marcognet's division coming up on the ridge, and the Greys, therefore, though previously ordered to act as a support, necessarily attacked direct to the Front. The cavalry had some difficulty in getting through Pack's brigade, all of which, except the left battalion which was ordered to remain on the crest, followed the horsemen as they went forward.

The Royal Dragoons struck with their centre squadron the leading column of Donzelot's division, which, being confronted by no troops, though it was under fire from the left of Kempt's brigade, was advancing with shouts of triumph across the ridge, when, within less than a hundred yards distance, it suddenly caught sight of the British cavalry, on which its front rank opened fire. About twenty Dragoons dropped from their saddles, but the "Royals" never drew rein, and the head of the French column, facing about, tried to get back on the other side of the hedges it had just crossed. In a moment the "Royals" were into the mass, sabring all those within reach, and, the rear battalions still coming on, the whole were presently so crowded together as to become absolutely helpless. Those in the centre of the column shot wildly in the air, while the bravest, coming out, engaged the Dragoons; many, however, throwing down their muskets, surrendered.

The "Royals" having slain many men, demoralised more, and taken an "Eagle," dashed on to the supporting columns; and presently, the Inniskillings having broken through Donzelot's rear demi-brigades, the entire French division fled, pursued by the Cavalry to the bottom of the valley. An officer visiting the scene next day saw on the slope rows of muskets which had been grounded in regular lines, indicating complete submission on the part of the main body of the vanquished before the mass broke up.

As the Scots Greys passed through the 92nd Regiment, each corps mutually cheered the other, and many of the Highlanders, by holding on to the stirrups, passed on with the horsemen as they rode into the head of Marcognet's column, which was utterly routed, Sergeant Ewart taking the "Eagle" of the 45th (French) regiment. The Greys then galloped on further for about three hundred yards against the supporting battalions, and, though a few of its outer files opened fire, our Dragoons, disregarding it, upset one of the columns. General Donzelot's entire Division, after the impact of the Inniskillings, was driven back, and although the rear column escaped notice at the moment, the Greys passing it on their left hand, many Frenchmen threw themselves on the ground, and when they arose offered to surrender.

The Inniskillings in the centre of the Union brigade galloped at the rear columns of Donzelot's division, composed of the 54th and 55th regiments, the right and centre squadrons attacking the 55th regiment, and the left squadron charging by itself the 54th regiment. The feeble fire from a few men in the front did not for a moment check the Inniskillings, who, riding into the middle of the ranks, struck down a number of men, while the remainder, throwing away their muskets, asked for, and received quarter. Some three thousand men were taken by Picton's men to the rear, as prisoners.

Ponsonby's three regiments then pressed on in an irregular line with Somerset's brigade, for the 1st Life Guards and two squadrons King's Dragoon Guards having passed round by the West and South sides of the farm, bringing up their right shoulders, pursued the Cuirassiers, many of whom were overtaken in the cutting immediately South of La Haie Sainte; others, however, were saved by Bachelu's infantry, who from either side of the summit of the cutting shot down many of the 1st Life Guards. The King's Dragoon Guards, passing between the 1st and 2nd Life Guards, rode up into the enemy's great battery, where they were joined by the 2nd Life Guards and by scattered parties of the Royals and Inniskillings; while still farther to the Eastward rode the Scots Greys, amongst whom some of the King's Dragoon Guards also were seen. As the Cavalry passed through the valley, they cut to pieces two field batteries, which, in trying to follow D'Erlon's corps had stuck fast in deep ground. Our men killed the gunners, drivers and teams, and destroyed the harness, wrecking fifteen guns so completely that they could not be brought into action again that day.

According to Prince De la Tour D'Auvergne's account, D'Erlon's disastrous attack cost the French 5000 men, killed, wounded or prisoners, two Eagles, and fifteen cannon wrecked. The English accounts state that detachments of the five cavalry regiments —for the Blues were kept together—rode about in the French battery on the ridge three hundred yards South of La Haie Sainte for some time, adding, if Supports had been at hand it might have been possible to have brought some of the guns away, for the French on the spot seemed to have temporarily lost all power of resistance. General Subervie, who hurried to the scene of action, used, in later years, to declare that unless the French cavalry had come up at this time, not a man of D'Erlon's infantry would have escaped.

Now, however, succour was at hand. Travers' brigade of Cuirassiers had been sent forward by General Milhaud ; a Lancer brigade was hurried up by General Jacquinot, and Napoleon himself came on the ridge as they returned after fully avenging D'Erlon's defeat on the scattered British dragoons.

While the Household and Union brigades were thus "crying Havoc" amidst the demoralised infantry of D'Erlon's Corps, they met with but little resistance from the "bewildered crowds of men." * When the Royal Dragoons charged Donzelot's division, some of

* 'Rassemblement confus.'—EDGAR QUINET.

those on the flanks of the mass faced inwards, and the rear battalion had already begun to retreat before a single Frenchman was struck, and this in spite of there being brave men among them, as is shown from many having run out to engage the Dragoons as they dashed into the mass of bewildered men. Not only were the columns sorely tried by the crowding together of the ranks, but when smitten by bullets, from hitherto unseen infantry, they were startled by the sudden rush of approaching Cavalry, and doubtless anticipated that those they saw would be followed by many squadrons, for such was the Continental custom.

What took place in Donzelot's division—horsemen hacking a confused and practically unresisting mob—occurred in different degrees in the other unwieldy, unmanageable masses. It is clear that the Regimental officers had no liking for such formations; for the officer commanding the Rear Echelon in Durutte's corps asked leave to modify it, but was told he "must obey orders." It was not only against Cavalry that these masses were ineffective. They were also useless opposed to troops in "extended order," for, although our skirmishers were driven in quickly by the Heads of the columns, yet individual British soldiers in retiring marched close to their flanks as they came on, firing into the crowded masses with impunity. No writer, so far as I know, has shown conclusively that this faulty formation was due to Ney, but the fact that he employed it at Borodino in 1812, and at Bautzen in 1813, indicates that he believed it to be the most suitable for raw troops. Napoleon at St. Helena condemned emphatically its use at Waterloo, and mentioned that it was the cause of the heavy loss of the French at Albuera. Jomini also says these unwieldy columns of D'Erlon's contributed greatly to the defeat of the Emperor's army on the 18th June, 1815.

There was only one demi-brigade intact after our Cavalry crossed the low ground between the two positions, and that was dispersed during the advance of Vandeleur's brigade, which I shall now describe; but before doing so it is desirable I should say that when Durutte, the leader of the Rear Echelon, advanced, he took forward six battalions only, leaving two on the Eastern flank of the great battery, which as I stated covered the advance of D'Erlon's Corps. Four battalions were sent against Smohain and Papelotte, and it appears that the other two battalions occupied the fields immediately to the Westward of those hamlets.

It is curious to read that Lord Uxbridge named a regiment in the Union brigade which he intended to act as Support, thus undertaking the work of a brigade Commander, but he gave no orders as to how far his cavalry might push on. When he saw that the greater part of the two brigades was completely beyond control, he and all the officers endeavoured to check the wild, disorderly gallop; in this, however, they had no success, except with the Regiments on the extreme right.

The Blues were intended to move in support of the 1st Brigade, but drew up into the front line before it passed the enclosures of La Haie Sainte, where Major Pack was killed. The Regiment was, however, kept well in hand, and under the protection of their solidly formed squadrons those men of the 1st Life Guards who escaped from the volleys of Bachelu's infantry, firing from the summit of the cutting South of La Haie Sainte, were enabled to effect a retreat. The 2nd Life Guards, and King's Dragoon Guards, who had gone right up into the French position, were fired on heavily by infantry, and were attacked by Travers' brigade of Milhaud's Cuirassier division. The Scots Greys, after entering the battery, wheeled to the left, pursuing their work of destruction to the Eastward, until they were menaced by the leading squadrons of Jacquinot's division of Lancers.

So great was the confusion in the French ranks,

that some of our men penetrated even to the second line, behind the Artillery waggons, and returned unscathed. This we learn from a trooper in the Household Brigade, who enjoyed several personal combats, and who described to Haydon, the Historical painter to whom he had, before the war, often sat as a model, how, far beyond the French guns, he came on some artillery drivers, mere boys, who sat crying on their horses. It may be difficult for those who have never seen a battle to understand how individual soldiers can ride with impunity inside the lines of a hostile army, but there were many instances at Balaclava (1854) of men of the Light Cavalry brigade returning safely after penetrating more than half a mile behind the Russian batteries.

Our officers at Waterloo were fully sensible of the opportunities they were offering to the enemy, and tried to keep their soldiers under control, sacrificing their lives in trying to do so, but they were not successful. An officer of the Scots Greys, in endeavouring to bring his men away from a column of French infantry which they were pursuing, was shot down by those in its ranks. Many other officers met their death in striving to rally their soldiers, and, like the colonels of the Scots Greys and King's Dragoon Guards, were slain within the French main position. As some of the

L

survivors said on their return, "If we could only have got a hundred men together, we could have got away."

The colonel of the Inniskilling Dragoons states distinctly that nobody was told how far they were to go, nor did he know which column his Regiment was to attack; and the want of clear orders excuses to some extent the lack of battle discipline amongst the Rank and File. This tendency, however, on the part of our Cavalry to break up in pursuit of the enemy, after a successful charge, had been noticed throughout the Peninsular War, both by French and English generals, and the Duke of Wellington held strong views on the subject.

Siborne writes that Lord Uxbridge at this time, seeing the Household and Union brigades scattered, looked round anxiously for the support of one of the Light brigades from the left of the position. I have already stated it does not appear that he had warned them of the attack he was about to make, and the brigade nearest at hand was commanded by a soldier who, however brave, was more accustomed to wait for orders than to act on his own initiative. He had served for a long time under the Duke of Wellington, and knew how heavily he could vent his displeasure on officers who moved without orders, for the whole

Peninsular army had felt the Duke's treatment of Norman Ramsay.*

When General Baron von Müffling, the Prussian military attaché, seeing what was about to occur, urged Vandeleur and Vivian to move to the support of the Union brigade, they both declined, saying, "Alas! we dare not move without orders," and Müffling eventually having left them before Vandeleur moved, remained for years under the impression that neither brigade had advanced. The brigadiers do not seem to have been aware that the Duke had put the cavalry entirely in Uxbridge's hands. His

* Ramsay, a model Horse-artilleryman, was a universal favourite, and much liked by Lord Wellington. When in temporary command of Major Bull's troop, at the battle of Vittoria, Ramsay had done well, and next day in the pursuit, Lord Wellington, after riding with the troop, personally ordered him to occupy a village for the night, saying if there were any orders in the course of the night he *would send them*. At 6 A.M. next day verbal orders were received for the troop to join its brigade, and after it had started a further written order was received from the Quartermaster-general to the same effect. Lord Wellington overtook the troop while Ramsay was away looking for the best road. He left orders for him to be placed under arrest, and he remained suspended from duty for a considerable time, his name being omitted from the Vittoria despatch, and this, in spite of the representations of Lord Fitzroy Somerset, Sir Thomas Graham, and many others. Lord Wellington maintained that he had said the troop was not to move without personal orders from him, but Ramsay and three others, who were present and heard his lordship speak, deny that these words were uttered.

ordship wrote in 1842 : "The Duke had placed the cavalry under me. . . . I received no order to make the first charge, nor any other during the day." There was, however, some ground for the brigadiers' apprehension of the Duke's displeasure, as is shown by his observation to Müffling, when discussing the question years afterwards, that he "would have tried either of them by court-martial had they moved, even if they were successful." This observation indicates that the Duke had forgotten Vandeleur's charge.

After Müffling had ridden away, Vandeleur changed his mind. His brigade was drawn up to the East of the Papelotte-Verd-Cocu road, which cuts through the ridge on which Wellington's army stood. To move directly South, and cross where the cutting was no longer an obstacle would have brought the brigade under close fire of Durutte's skirmishing line, and so Vandeleur turned Northwards for about a quarter of a mile, and came back to the Front through Best's Hanoverians ; but by this time the Scots Greys had suffered great loss, and the commander of the Union brigade had been killed. After Sir William Ponsonby had crossed the valley, the hack he was riding, being exhausted, could not move faster than a walk, and seeing a squadron of Jacquinot's Lancers approaching, he took a locket off his neck and gave it to his Aide-de-camp, who was better mounted, with instructions that he should, if he escaped, ensure its reaching Lady Ponsonby. Both officers were, however, speared, as were many of those overtaken in the low ground.

When Vandeleur's brigade at last came over the ridge, the 12th Light Dragoons, leading, saw in their front that the only remaining intact column (46th Regiment) of Marcognet's division was moving back steadily and in order. The scattered men of the Union brigade were being followed so closely by some Lancers, that the order was given to the 12th Light Dragoons, "Squadrons right half wheel, charge." The 46th Regiment attempted to stand when the Dragoons were seen approaching, but being caught on its right flank it broke up, and the 12th, galloping right through the crowd, without pausing to re-form, struck into the flank of some squadrons of Jacquinot's Lancers.

Just before this happened, as the 12th charged down the slope the smoke was so thick that it was difficult to tell friends from foes, and the Regiment suffered more from the bullets of Pack's brigade in its right rear than from Durutte's skirmishers on the left flank. The 12th and 16th Dragoons came also under artillery fire from the French position, but this was more destructive to Jacquinot's Lancers than to our men. Colonel Frederick Ponsonby of the 12th was first wounded in both arms, and then was struck down by sword-cuts on the head, dealt by men following him. He fell on his face, and while on the ground was speared by a Lancer—for no quarter was given, nor even asked for, in this part of the field—but after being left for dead, he was eventually brought in next day, and recovered.

While the 12th Light Dragoons, having wheeled into line, were riding through the French infantry, higher up the hill, and nearer to the British position, the 16th Light Dragoons, led by Vandeleur, caught the head of Jacquinot's Lancers in their front, but somewhat obliquely. The two British regiments then drove the enemy to the foot of the valley beyond which Vandeleur had ordered his men not to go. Some few of each Regiment did, however, ascend the opposite height, where they were overwhelmed by the French cavalry, which had then arrived in force. The 12th Light Dragoons, caught in disorder when pursuing, broke up in the valley, and were soon overtaken by other squadrons of the Lancers then coming on the ground.

Although Jacquinot's men spared neither effective nor wounded men, Travers' brigade of Milhaud's Cuirassiers acted differently. One of them galloped at a trumpeter with the intention of running him through, but, seeing how young the boy was, dropped the point of his sword and passed on, but was almost immediately killed by a 2nd Life Guardsman, who had not noticed that he had spared the lad.

It is pleasant to record another case of generous conduct, which, happily, was rewarded. Major Poten of the King's German Legion, having lost his right arm in the Peninsula, was attended by two non-commissioned officers at Waterloo, who were detailed to ride one on either side of him. In the confusion of a charge during the afternoon they were, however, separated from the Major, and he was attacked by a Cuirassier, who had already raised his sword when the Major, turning his horse, showed that he had no right arm, and the Frenchman, dropping the point of his sword to "the salute," rode away. After the arrival of the Allied armies in Paris, Major Poten accidentally met his merciful antagonist, and seeking out the colonel of the regiment, reported the incident to him. The French soldier received the Cross of the Legion of Honour.*

The survivors of the Heavy cavalry now drew back, the retreat of the Union brigade being covered to some extent by Vandeleur's brigade, and a regiment

* From "Bismark's Cavalry," translated by Beamish.

of Dutch-Belgian cavalry, which advanced about half way down the slope to the valley.

The British squadrons re-formed on the position they had previously occupied, but D'Erlon's disorganised corps was withdrawn out of sight to the Southward of "La Belle Alliance." The crowd of shouting and fighting men disappeared, and no troops remained on the slopes on which Wellington's Staff had witnessed one of the most brilliant successes ever achieved by Horsemen over Infantry.

No reader, however careful, would gather from any British authors I have studied, except perhaps from the writings of Sir Hussey Vivian, that two brigades had wrecked an infantry Corps and some of its Artillery so completely, that its Infantry never came forward again till late in the day, and then with perceptibly lessened ardour. Jomini, and other Frenchmen indeed, as I have said, estimated properly the practical worth of these charges, but no one, however, who has perused the vast library of English literature on Waterloo, can have failed to notice how comparatively little credit is given by Englishmen to the British cavalry for its work on June 18th. We have only to compare the despatch with the description of the elation felt by the Duke of Wellington's Staff on seeing the glorious results obtained by the Household and Union brigades, to realise the feeling thus described by a Cavalry officer who greatly distinguished himself on June 17th :—

"*July 1st*, 1815.
"BEFORE PARIS.
"The whole army cry out against Lord Wellington's despatch. It is the coldest and most flat production that even his lordship ever produced."

I should state it seems doubtful whether the Duke of Wellington saw the actual charge of the Union brigade, as he was, I believe, to the Westward of the Genappe-Brussels road at the time, and the fact of Sir William Ponsonby being killed, and also of Lord Uxbridge having led the Household brigade, militated against the Union brigade charge being appreciated at its real worth.

Ney, about 3 P.M., seriously attacked La Haie Sainte, which, according to the French accounts, was captured between 3.30 and 4 o'clock, though Major Baring alleges that he and his few surviving men did not vacate the dwelling-house—*i.e.*, that nearest to the British position—till shortly before 6 o'clock.

It is doubtful whether the brave Germans would ever have been driven out if their ammunition had not failed. Some writers have reflected, but as it seems to me, unjustly, on Wellington's want of arrangement in allowing such a failure to occur. As the Infantry battalions stood in one position for eight hours, it was easy to supply them with ammunition, and this was done in all other cases, a cartload being in one instance put down inside a square during one of the cavalry attacks. Major Baring's battalion, however, had a special rifle, and the carts containing the reserve ammunition for it went astray during a panic about 2 P.M., being finally upset in a ditch. The confusion as to the hour at which the post was captured arises, I believe, from the French writers regarding the capture of the farm as accomplished when its defenders could no longer harass their columns, which were preparing to assault the right centre of the British position; whereas English writers attach greater importance to our hold of the most Northern building of La Haie Sainte being maintained, so as to prevent the French concentrating close under our main position, as they did about 7 P.M. Baring's men had naturally paid most attention to loopholing the Southern end of the farm buildings; and thus, when they were driven back to the dwelling-house, it was difficult for them to fire on to the French troops standing immediately West of the farm.

MARSHAL NEY.

Third Attack.

About 4 P.M. Ney commenced a series of cavalry attacks on the Allied right wing; and the whole of the serious fighting from this time till the final advance of the British troops took place on the open space of nine hundred yards lying between the enclosures of La Haie Sainte and Hougomont. On this confined ground Ney led forward Milhaud's corps of Cuirassiers, 21 squadrons, and the Light cavalry of the Guard, 19 squadrons, in all some

4500 men. Now a man on horseback occupies about one yard in the ranks, and as in order to ensure mobility it is necessary to have some interval between squadrons, it is clear that there was but very little space for this number of horsemen.

Some French writers say there were twenty squadrons in the first line. This is obviously impossible. Colonel Sir Shaw-Kennedy, an eye-witness, says the necessity of avoiding the fire from the outposts in the arms contracted the available space for the advance to five hundred yards; but we know that fire from La Haie Sainte had not prevented cavalry remaining close under its Western enclosure since 2 P.M., and some French squadrons certainly passed close to Hougomont. I believe the frontage of the attacking horsemen varied from four to eight squadrons, being mainly influenced by the slopes of the ground (see the diagrams page 157).

The fire of the French artillery was well maintained prior to the advance of the cavalry, all their available batteries being brought forward. The Allied infantry were ordered to lie down behind the crest of the ridge, and were thus to some extent saved from the iron shower which tore frightful gaps through battalions when it did strike them; but the soft condition of the ground neutralised many of the projectiles. The

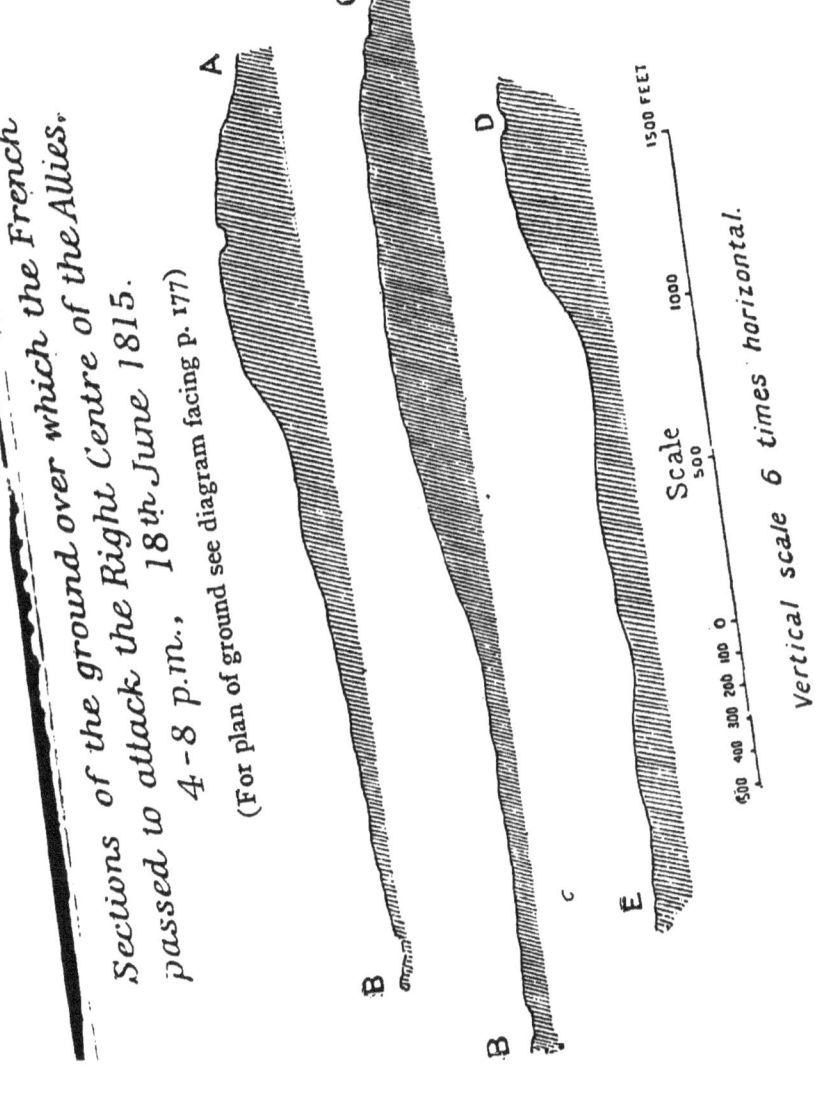

Sections of the ground over which the French passed to attack the Right Centre of the Allies, 4-8 p.m., 18th June 1815.

(For plan of ground see diagram facing p. 177)

Allied artillerymen, both British and German, stood up to their guns until the Cavalry actually reached them, when, "by order," they ran back, and lay down under the bayonets of the squares. This order did not reach some batteries, in which both the officers and men remained with their guns.

After a demonstration (mentioned lower down) by Piré's Light Cavalry to the Westward of Hougomont —which was, however, but feebly carried out—the forty squadrons having got into position between the Genappe-Brussels road and the South-East corner of Hougomont, advanced, the British infantry running into square at the same time.

According to the French historians, there was not one of the Cuirassiers who was not fully confident that he was going forward to complete a victory which had been practically already decided. The British infantry were not visible, and they were believed to be already in full retreat. Thus the immense mass advanced, full of confidence, and without a single squadron of the two Cavalry Corps being held in Reserve. They moved at first at a slow trot; and, while their artillery necessarily ceased fire, the British batteries, though firing as rapidly as possible, could scarcely miss the enormous target. As the first line of Cuirassiers came on, all wearing breastplates, they produced a magnificent scenic effect; and though there were soon gaps made through the ranks, no one wavered. When the leading squadrons approached nearer, the guns of the Allies were double-loaded with shot and canister, and some of them were fired with the muzzles actually touching men and horses, ere the gunners ran back to the infantry squares, leaving, in many instances, four and five dead Cuirassiers heaped together, but still in the saddle on their lifeless horses.

The 1st line of squadrons having mounted the crest, their trumpeters sounded the gallop, and they disappeared momentarily from the sight of those following them, who imagined that the first line had carried all in front of it. This was not the case: instead of a retreating infantry, there stood, as if rooted in the ground, some 6000 men—the 3rd British Division—ranged in two lines of nine squares,* the four in second line being opposite to the intervals of the first row. On the left of the 3rd Division stood a brigade of Brunswick troops, and on the right Maitland's brigade of Guards. Behind the infantry stood the remnants of the Heavy cavalry, Grant's, and Dörnberg's Light cavalry brigades.

As the Cuirassiers advanced against the squares,

* In reality "oblongs."

not a musket was fired until they came within thirty paces. It then generally happened that the head of the squadrons, struck down by leaden hail, fell—in some instances, no doubt, horses knocked down our men in the squares—and the formation was temporarily broken; but as the French officers said with admiring astonishment, in that, the first, as in most of the subsequent attacks, the British infantry never moved till they got the command "Close up,"* when they re-formed without the slightest hesitation.

Generally, when the leading horsemen fell, those behind them opened out to the right and left, and, passing on, received from the flank of the squares a still more deadly fire. The Duke of Wellington, in writing to General Beresford on July 2nd, 1815, observed: "We had the French cavalry walking about us for some time as if they had been our own;" and this observation, although his Lordship did not probably so mean it, expresses, so I understand, exactly the situation during these attacks. They *walked* about but did not *charge* the squares. The French officers showed the most devoted gallantry. One who, with desperate valour, penetrated a square, lay sorely wounded on the ground, and begged our soldiers to kill him. This they

* " Serrez les rangs."

CHARGE OF THE FRENCH CUIRASSIERS AT WATERLOO.

refused to do; and, intensely mortified by his men's failure to follow him, he took his own life. The French privates were courageous enough, but not sufficiently trained to follow their leaders closely, and were thus incapable of making vigorous concerted attacks. Lord Uxbridge says that they charged without any vigour or dash, having lost heart from the occurrences two hours previously. There does not seem to be adequate ground for this opinion, as with the exception of Dubois' brigade of two regiments, the only cavalry engaged before 4 P.M. had enjoyed an easy victory in slaughtering the scattered and breathless men of the Union brigade. I attribute the failure of the attempt to break our soldiers' ranks, to want of training: to the French officers being strangers to the men: and to the courage and discipline of our Infantry.

Although the Regiments of the Imperial Guard were for some time on the British plateau, yet they never galloped either in overwhelming masses, or even in a formed body, on to the bayonets of our infantry. Every attack was made in column, and not even one in line: individuals rode up to our men and strove to knock aside the bayonets, but only with the result that their bodies and those of their horses soon formed ramparts round the square. Successive regiments coming up got mixed, not merely in squadrons, but by regiments and corps. They were now charged by the British cavalry and driven off the plateau, on the upper slopes of which, however, our horsemen generally remained. One regiment, however, the men of which, forgetful of the orders they had received, went down into the valley, and being surrounded by hostile horsemen, suffered considerably, losing also some men from the fire of British infantry, who mistook our Dragoons for the enemy.

The French cavalry, re-forming under the British position, repeated their attack, this time, however, holding back a portion of their third line to meet the British squadrons; but after a time the French were again driven to the low ground. During one of these attacks, Lord Uxbridge led a squadron of Household Cavalry against a huge French cavalry column, and arrested its progress though he failed to drive it back.

Though the French squadrons were unable to remain within sight of our infantry or guns, they merely withdrew below the crest, and individuals menaced the guns whenever an attempt was made to reload them. Major Lloyd, with one gunner of his battery, succeeded in firing six rounds into the serried mass, the head-dress of which he could just see; but he was interrupted again and again when about to fire by an officer of the Imperial Guard, who, though alone, rode straight at the Major several times when he was reloading. A Brunswick rifleman shot the Frenchman; but eventually the Major was mortally wounded by another of these indomitable and devoted officers.

Fourth Attack.

Ney prepared another attack of cavalry with the survivors of the previous continuous charges. To support them, he formed up Kellerman's division, consisting of 11 squadrons of Cuirassiers, 7 of Dragoons, and 6 of Carabiniers and Guyot's division of Heavy Cavalry of the Guards, consisting of 6 squadrons Horse Grenadiers and 7 of Dragoons: in all a reinforcement of 37 squadrons. We should bear in mind that the ground was now encumbered with numberless corpses of men and horses.

Kellerman, who really understood the employment of cavalry, kept back the brigade of Carabiniers (1000 strong), and endeavoured to retain it out of Ney's sight. He had left this brigade in order to lead the Cuirassiers, when Ney, looking round, caught sight of the Carabiniers, and galloping back, reproached the brigadier, took his brigade forward, and thus succeeded in again bringing on every available squadron, without holding one in Reserve. Kellerman saw from a distance what Ney was doing, and endeavoured to stop the advance of the Carabiniers, but was too late. Seventy-seven squadrons were thus led forward, this time the deepest part of the mass being taken farther Westwards, *i.e.* nearer Hougomont.

The crowd of horsemen came on under the concentrated fire of the British guns, and the same scenes were renewed again and again. The bravest and best trained of these gallant Frenchmen fell on the bayonets of our infantry, but their successors wheeled round on either side of the squares, incurring greater danger than if they had resolutely followed their leaders. Some, however, pushed on to the ammunition wagons far down the Northern slope on the reverse side of the British position, and there killed drivers and horses.

One squadron of the 1st Cuirassiers having got far in advance did not retire with the rest of its brigade, but breaking through the centre of the Allied infantry endeavoured to rejoin the left of the French army. In nearly all the English narratives,* credit is taken for the destruction or capture of the entire squadron, but in a French account there is a vivid description of

* See, for instance, p. 167.

how after the bursting forth of a blaze of musketry to the Westward of Hougomont, out of the smoke appeared, led by a subaltern, a band of fifteen breathless men who had succeeded in breaking through the British line. Three officers, eighty Non-commissioned officers and men of the squadron, were killed and wounded; it had numbered about 120 when it first charged.

General Lord Hill, an eye-witness, thus described the destruction of these gallant soldiers :—" Four times were our guns in possession of their (French) cavalry, and as often did the bayonets of our infantry rescue them. For upwards of an hour our little squares were surrounded by the *élite* of the French cavalry : they gallantly stood within forty paces of us, unable to leap over the bristling line of bayonets, unwilling to retire, and determined never to surrender. Hundreds of them were dropping in all directions from our murderous fire, yet as fast as they dropped others came up to supply their places. Finding at last it was in vain to attempt to break our determined ranks, they swept round our rear and, rushing into the Nivelles road, attempted to cut their way back to their own lines ; but the whole road was lined with our infantry on both sides, and the advanced part of it was an almost impassable barricade of felled trees. Here fell the remainder of these gallant Cuirassiers of whom not one was taken prisoner without first of all being wounded."

The 5th Light Cavalry brigade consisted of the 7th Hussars, 13th Light Dragoons, and 15th Hussars under command of Major-General Sir Colquhoun Grant. It was posted near the junction of the Nivelles-Wavre roads, about half of the 15th Hussars being on outpost to the extreme West of the position. Between 3 and 4 P.M., the 13th Light Dragoons and 15th Hussars were sent to the right to meet a threatened attack by ten squadrons of Piré's Lancers, who were supported by 12 guns. The Lancers, however, retired with the guns on the advance of the 5th brigade, and General Grant, hearing the cheering of Piré's men who shouted on seeing an attack of the Cuirassiers on the main position, left one squadron out on the right flank and returned to the rear of Hougomont where his brigade had been previously formed under cover. He had scarcely reached his original ground when the 13th Light Dragoons, forming line to the front, charged a body of Cuirassiers, and drove them back about 300 yards. The 15th Hussars charged on the left of the 13th with a similar success, while the 7th Hussars made a brilliant attack on a regiment of Lancers, which came on in three distinct bodies, formed slightly in echelon. These charges were renewed again and again, the 13th having eventually only one squadron remaining out of the three which had paraded in the morning.

The 7th Hussars and 23rd Light Dragoons also made many charges during the afternoon, the result being always so far satisfactory to the British troops that in all cases the French squadrons were finally driven off the crest of the position. The fighting was hand to hand, and one officer, Lieutenant Uniacke of the 7th Hussars, after having three horses killed under him, finished the day's work on the horse of a French Cuirassier officer whom he had killed in a personal encounter. There were many instances similar to that of this gallant Hussar, but unfortunately in few cases has there been any record published of personal incidents during the hardest fighting of the Cavalry engagements, although we know there are private letters of interest which have never been made public. Thus we learn, from a letter to Mrs. Uniacke, the officer's mother, what happened to her son's first charger, of the fate of which he gave a very vivid description, showing the intensity of the fire under which our Cavalry acted. In a struggle with an officer of the Imperial

Guard, Uniacke's horse received a heavy cut over the face, and was shortly afterwards shot through the neck. As the rider dismounted, the unfortunate horse's lower jaw was taken off by a cannon ball, which put an end to its sufferings; but the lieutenant was no sooner up on a troop horse than a shell, exploding underneath the animal's forelegs, killed it outright. The 7th Hussars suffered heavily in the two days' fighting, for going into action with 24 officers and 352 of all other ranks, they had 12 officers and 151 of all other ranks killed or wounded.

Ney led or sent forward the cavalry twelve times, and, according to the accounts of French officers, in the later attacks their squadrons were better handled than in the earlier advances; but the final result was identical with that of the previous charges. This failure is not astonishing, as these later attacks were generally carried out at the walk. The men in the Cuirassiers were magnificent in stature; the Regiments had been made up from Mounted police,* and draughts of thirty picked men from each dragoon regiment in the service; but they had not worked together even in squadrons, and half the horses had only been recently purchased.

Slowly and most reluctantly the exhausted horse-

* "Gens d'armes."

men fell back and re-formed in line between La Haie Sainte and Hougomont, whence they had started. They had left two-thirds of their numbers strewed on the plateau and slopes of the ridge, nearly all the Field officers being killed or wounded, and the few who were unscathed by sword or bullet, had been seriously hurt by the pressure in the mass of horses.

Under cover of the cavalry attacks, the infantry of Quiot's (Alix) division, pressing forward, endeavoured to surround Baring's men, who were holding the garden North of the dwelling-house of La Haie Sainte ; and the Prince of Orange, to extricate them, ordered down the 5th and 8th battalions, of Ompteda's brigade, under Colonel Schröder ; these deploying, charged across the hollow road, and drove the enemy before them. They were however immediately caught in flank by a body of Cuirassiers, who were close under the crest. The 5th battalion was succoured in time by the remnants of Somerset's Household cavalry, but the 8th battalion, being farther in advance and to the left, was cut down and dispersed, losing its colonel and several officers, as well as a Colour. Later, after Baring had abandoned La Haie Sainte, the French infantry lining the Southern edge of the crest poured a hot fire into the Allied squares, and the 27th Inniskillings, standing

immediately North of the cross roads, in a short time
lost half their numbers, but without flinching or
moving from the spot! The enduring courage of this
Regiment was remarkable even amongst the many
heroic deeds performed that day. The battalion
having been quartered at Ghent had marched thence,
without halting for more than a few minutes, to
Mont St. Jean, the village North of Waterloo, where
the men slept soundly from 9 A.M. till 3 P.M., when
they took post in the position to close an open gap.
When towards the end of the battle the French
occupied the knoll above the Sandpit near La Haie
Sainte, they fired into the Inniskillings with such
effect that eventually two-thirds of the battalion fell.
The survivors of a battalion of Kielmannsegge's
brigade stood equally firm under the following
similarly trying circumstances. The French succeeded in bringing two guns into action to the North-
West of La Haie Sainte, within 300 yards of the
Allied line, and before they could be driven back
fired two or three rounds at the square, blowing
away one face of it. The Prince of Orange now
ordered Brigadier-General Ompteda to deploy and
advance against the enemy's infantry then coming on.
Though this brave and accomplished officer pointed
out to the Aide-de-Camp who brought the order that

the French cavalry were immediately under the crest, the Prince, after hearing his expostulation, disregarded the warning, ordering him to be silent and obey. He at once deployed the 5th battalion and charged. The French infantry drew back, and a

WILLIAM PRINCE OF ORANGE.

regiment of Cuirassiers, catching Ompteda's men in flank, rolled them up from right to left, killing the Brigadier, and destroying the battalion; thirty effectives only answered the muster-roll after this unfortunate attack. The Prince, who, though an incompetent soldier, was a brave man, shortly after Ompteda's death led forward another battalion himself, and was wounded. This wound was fortunate for his reputation, as it doubtless tended to make people forget he was the direct cause of the loss of the 69th British Regiment on the 16th, and Ompteda's two battalions sacrificed on the 18th June.

Fifth Attack.

Now, at last, soon after five o'clock the heads of the Prussian cavalry brigades were approaching the left of the Allied position, the Infantry having got into action somewhat sooner, near Planchenoit. The 4th Corps (Bulow) had been "under arms" ever since 4 A.M., but its main body did not reach St. Lambert till noon, where it halted for some time four or five miles from Planchenoit.

Until von Ollech's history of the campaign of 1815 was published in 1876, the delay of the Prussian Army to come to the assistance of the Allies had been put down to the difficulties of the roads, which were admittedly great, and to the fact of a fire having broken out in the street of Wavre at 5.30 in the morning, which also doubtless impeded the march through that place. There were, however, six bridges within three and a half miles, and von Ollech leaves no uncertainty at all as to the primary cause of the tardy assistance afforded by our Allies.

Field-Marshal Blücher was very anxious to move, but his Chief-of-the-Staff was fully persuaded that the Duke of Wellington had "left him in the lurch" at Ligny, and had broken his promise that he would support the Prussians. Von Gneisenau argued: "If the English only make a demonstration with a Rearguard and then fall back on Brussels, we shall be caught in making a flank march in a difficult country, and have the whole weight of the French army on us;" and it was not until the sound of the heavy fire, opened about 12 o'clock, reached the ears of the Prussian Chief-of-Staff, that he felt persuaded the English meant to fight on their ground, and that he decided to throw the whole strength of the Army into the struggle.

The Duke of Wellington does not seem to have greatly appreciated the value of cavalry for the Waterloo position, for his first demand for assistance was for 3000 infantry,* or quite literally "3000 men," without specifying what Arm of the Service he most required. This request was refused, the Prussian commander saying he could not make a detachment as his whole force was coming up into action. It is

---

* A striking fact when we remember there were 18,000 men standing idle at Hal, eight miles to the Westward.

obvious that when, at 12 o'clock, the heads of Grouchy's column were still distant, that a much-needed reinforcement of Prussian cavalry could easily have reached the left of the British position two and a half hours before they actually arrived. It is only right to add that the Duke of Wellington's first message, that he would fight if only one Prussian corps were sent to his assistance, did not indicate any anticipation of being greatly pressed.

Soon after 5.30 the Prussian cavalry came up on Vivian's left, to the North of Papelotte ; and he, hearing of the stress in the centre of Wellington's position, suggested to Vandeleur, his senior officer, that the two brigades should move Westwards. Vandeleur declined to stir without orders ; so Vivian decided to take his own brigade to the centre of the position, and had got near the Genappe-Brussels road, when he met Lord Uxbridge, who was coming to bring both brigades to support the infantry near La Haie Sainte. And this support was sorely needed. It was near La Haie Sainte that the French made their most successful efforts, and if we compare the terrible losses suffered by the Inniskilling Fusiliers[*] and those of the 52nd Light Infantry[†]

[*] 478 casualties out of a total strength of 698.
[†] 38 killed and 168 wounded out of an effective strength of over 1000.

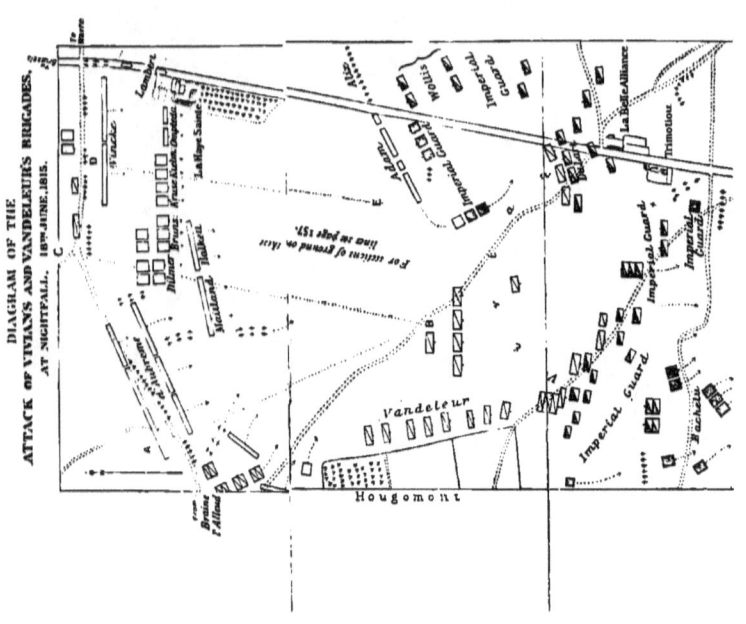

posted partly under cover of Hougomont, we shall realise the great importance of maintaining these outworks to the main position. When Vivian got near the cross-roads, seeing but two weak squadrons of Heavy cavalry, he asked Lord Edward Somerset, "Where is your brigade?" And he pointed to those few then in the saddles! For the next two hours these devoted squadrons, formed in single rank, filled up the gap in the infantry line, and thus encouraged some of the half-trained soldiers of our Allies to stand firm. Before nightfall the survivors of the seven Heavy regiments of the 1st, and Union brigades were re-formed into one squadron of only fifty files.

When Sir Hussey Vivian arrived at the centre of the position, the scene of ruin in the vicinity of the cross-roads showed no indication of the coming victory. Hundreds of men, dead and dying, were lying on the ridge, while numberless loose and mutilated horses wandered in circles, bewildered by the smoke and deafening noise of the guns. There the two cavalry brigades stood till, the attack of the Imperial Guard having failed, Adams' brigade, on the initiative of Colborne of the 52nd, by striking into the flank of these renowned soldiers, pushed them gradually back past La Haie Sainte. Then the Guard divided, as did Adams' brigade—a portion of it going up either side of the Genappe road, driving all before it.'

When the Duke of Wellington saw the Imperial Guard go back, he ordered Vivian to the Front; and he was followed in the right rear by Vandeleur, who moved close along the Eastern border of Hougomont, while Vivian descended the slope covered by dead and dying cavalry men. The smoke at this time hanging over the ground was so thick that Vivian could see nothing; but from the fire and the shouting farther to the Eastward it was apparent that the French were falling back. When the brigade got to the low ground, the brigadier saw in front of him crowds of scattered fugitives, and two or three squares of well-formed infantry, flanked on either side by Cavalry and Artillery. As is natural under the circumstances, the accounts as to the composition of these squares differ materially, but all writers agree that the cavalry near them were the remnants of the squadrons which had been so recklessly squandered between 4 and 6 P.M. Though some French authors assert that the infantry squares were the shaken remnants of Quiot's and Donzelot's division, the Emperor's account appears to put the matter beyond dispute, for in his published gazette* he said: "Just as night fell, four battalions

* "Bulletin."

of the Middle Guard were charged in flank by several British squadrons, and put in disorder. The fugitives ran back, and others, seeing troops of the Guard flying, thought it was the Old Guard, and the panic spread immediately over the whole of the battlefield."

As Vivian, having formed line on his leading squadron, was advancing to attack, he received an order not to charge Infantry unless he felt sure of breaking the squares. He urged, however, that the enemy's cavalry, if unmolested, might charge our infantry; and he led the 10th Hussars against a regiment of Lancers which formed the left of the French horsemen. A squadron of Cuirassiers attempted to arrest the advance, but was beaten back. The French Carabiniers, charging our cavalry skirmishers, came under infantry fire at fifty paces and were destroyed, and the three squadrons of the 10th, each riding into distinct bodies of the enemy, put to flight all the mounted men to the Westward of the infantry squares. Vivian, ordering the 10th to re-form, galloped back to the 18th Hussars, being attacked on his way by a Cuirassier. Although Vivian had but one hand,* he managed to wound his antagonist, who was killed by the orderly following the General. Riding up to the 18th, he

* See page 112.

shouted, " 18th, you will follow me ? " and was answered by Sergeant-Major Jeffs : " Yes, General, to hell if you will lead us," and the Hussars galloped forward with great determination. As they pressed on, a battery of artillery crossed their front, and was ridden over and destroyed. Without a check, the 18th, after having first upset some squadrons in their immediate front, inclined to the right, on to a body of horsemen who were covering the retirement of one of the squares, which was now falling back. The French squadrons were driven away, and a battery behind them was abandoned by its detachments, all of them flying in disorder. Two squares, however, of the Old Guard were still intact.

As the 18th were re-forming, General Vivian rode back for the supporting regiment—the 1st King's German Legion—and he came on a weak squadron of the 10th Hussars standing near one of the squares of the Old Guard. While discussing the situation with Major Howard, who commanded the squadron, some of whose men were falling from the fire of the front rank of the square, they saw a British battalion approaching on their left flank with the apparent intention of attacking, and the General thereupon ordered the squadron to attack. It charged absolutely up to the Frenchmen's bayonets, on to which

Major Howard, shot in three places, literally fell; but the British battalion passed on without attacking, and although Howard's men would not leave the square, fighting desperately with individuals, yet they failed to break it. The square was shaken, however, and, after some hand-to-hand fighting, these grand veterans fell slowly back to the Genappe road.

Vandeleur's brigade, under command of Colonel Sleigh—for Vandeleur had succeeded to the command of the cavalry on Uxbridge being wounded, which happened just as the British infantry advanced—passed on farther to the Westward, and attacked a large square of infantry between Mon Plaisir and Rossomme, breaking it up, and making many prisoners. This square had, however, been previously dispersed, but rallying had got together again. The 16th Dragoons came on a large body of French infantry endeavouring to form square, and, charging it, took or destroyed the entire column; while almost at the same moment the 11th Light Dragoons, farther to the Westward, took a battery—the last of the French guns in position. Our cavalry were now careering amongst crowds of fugitives, and our Leaders behaved with great humanity, for an officer who was there heard the order given to spare the drivers of a battery of Horse artillery which had been surrounded.

Some few of the Imperial Guard attempted to bayonet individual officers; and the orderly of the officer commanding the 18th, in order to save his colonel, was compelled to cut down six in succession. There was, however, practically no further general resistance, except from the Grenadiers-à-Cheval of the Guard, who absolutely declined to surrender. They were covering a square in which Napoleon and his Staff had taken shelter, and no efforts, until darkness fell, could drive them away faster than a foot's pace. Inside that devoted band, around the Emperor, rode Soult, Bertrand, Brouat, Corbinau, Flahaut, and Gorgaud. It was at first Napoleon's intention to stop with the square, but Soult recognising the impossibility of further resistance, seized the bridle of the Emperor's horse, and dragged him away saying, "Your Majesty! Are not they already successful enough?" and the Emperor rode off, at first across fields, towards Charleroi.

Vivian's and Vandeleur's brigades halted about 10 P.M., but the Prussian and Brunswick cavalry pressed the retreating French throughout the night. From nine distinct, and separate bivouacs the demoralised soldiers were driven, and when the light of the moon was insufficient to enable their pursuers to see to kill men, the sound of a Prussian drum, carried on a troop horse, was sufficient to goad the fugitives into renewed efforts to escape. These poor creatures, many wounded and all wearied, attempted a last stand at Genappe, where about eight hundred were slaughtered, and every gun then on the road was taken. There was little or no resistance, but no cessation of slaughter! At Charleroi Napoleon himself, about 5 A.M. on the 19th, attempted to stop the flight of his troops, but in vain. Beyond the town there are two roads which separate, and the greater part of the fugitives followed that leading to Avesnes, while others fled towards Phillippeville.

We get a vivid description of the horrors of this night from Foy's Aide-de-Camp, Captain Delafosse. At the end of the battle, in the fast falling night, a group of General and Staff officers came together under a hedge on the South side of the Hougomont enclosure, amongst whom were Generals Reille (whose horse was just then shot under him), D'Erlon, Bachelu, Jamin, and Foy. Three hundred men were all that remained of Foy's division. Three Generals had been killed close to the spot. Foy himself had been shot through the shoulder; and the whole of his Staff, except two, had been killed or wounded.

Delafosse's horse was now shot, and while an orderly was trying to find him another, the Aide-de-Camp took a half loaf out of the knapsack of a dead soldier, which he eagerly devoured, having eaten nothing for two days ; this was very much the general condition of all the men and horses, at all events, of the Staff. The horse killed under Delafosse had not been fed, or even unbridled since early on the 17th June.

Foy's party eventually reached the Bois de Bossu, on the Quatre Bras battlefield, where the 300 men halted while Delafosse tried to cross the road to obtain orders for the Retreat, but the crowd of fugitives carried him away, and he had some difficulty in getting over to the farm of Quatre Bras. There he found General Lobau asleep, and where he was shortly afterwards taken prisoner. Delafosse got back to his General who was now alone, for having become impatient he had incautiously approached the road, where his men, mingling with the other fugitives, joined in the general Retreat.

What this became is nearly indescribable, but if my readers would realise what a beaten, flying, and demoralised army becomes when all bonds of discipline are dissolved, let them imagine a torrent composed of terror-stricken men rushing along in irresistible force. Now and again a broken vehicle, a foundered horse, or a falling wounded comrade, arrests momentarily

FLIGHT FROM WATERLOO.

the onward rush, but the surging stream at once broadens out, and its increased weight presses down the delaying object, which, if animate, is quickly trampled to death. As General von Gneisenau wrote to his wife next day, "the road resembled a sea-shore strewn with cannons, limbers, muskets, ammunition and baggage wagons, wreckage of all descriptions."

General Foy and four officers still with him got together a corporal and 4 dragoons as escort, and eventually they arrived at Vieville, about 15 miles to the Westward of the line of Retreat, and then, retracing their steps, reached Marchiennes at six o'clock in the morning of the 19th June. Ney was there, but completely worn out and asleep, and Foy and his companions rode on towards Beaumont. Twelve miles North of Beaumont they came on a strong body of French cavalry retreating. When near the town, this column saw coming out of a wood to the Eastward a body of cavalry wearing green dolmans. It was their own 8th Hussar Regiment, but the column was so demoralised, that on a shout being raised, "Prussian cavalry," the whole galloped off, though ten times as strong as the supposed enemy, crushing every one in its flight. The infantry in Beaumont were plundering the private houses, and one man whom Delafosse tried to arrest endeavoured to bayonet the Staff officer.

All these incidents indicate that far from the French Army beaten by the Allies being the finest ever led by Napoleon, it was wanting in that first quality discipline, which, under the most favourable circumstances, cannot be acquired in three months, and which, moreover, had just then been weakened in the strongest link of discipline's chain, that is, fidelity to its oath of obedience.

Modern cavalry soldiers who read these pages will be astonished to find how, in leading charges, the generals displaced the commanding officers. Vivian went so far as to halt his second line (the 18th) till he could charge with the first line (the 10th) and return to lead the 18th. He only failed to lead the 3rd Regiment owing to the darkness preventing further attacks being executed.

Lord Uxbridge made but one mistake, and that was, undertaking a brigadier-general's and even a squadron leader's duties in the first charge. For this there was absolutely no excuse. Siborne urges that the General wished to excite the courage of his men. This is absurd. The Life Guards required no example to make them fight, and their brigadier, Lord Edward

Somerset, had made his mark at Salamanca (1812). Lord Uxbridge himself, writing in 1839, points out his "great mistake in having led the attack of the Household brigade." It induced nearly all the loss incurred, for the Union brigade had scarcely any casualties till their men retreated from the French battery; and if Lord Uxbridge had remained behind near Wellington's tree on the cross-roads, and sent Vandeleur's brigade down the slope at once, most of the men of the Union brigade on their exhausted horses would have got back safely. This was, however, his lordship's only fault throughout the day in which he showed great skill, initiative, and the most daring courage. He by no means contented himself with leading cavalry brigades. Several times in the afternoon he rallied infantry of the Allies which had been crushed by artillery fire—and at a critical moment he led a single squadron against a massive column, and, though the men did not follow up, he reached, and struck the enemy's bayonets with his sword ere he turned.

I do not pretend to have alluded to all the charges delivered during the battle, but only to such as give soldiers lessons for the future. So far as I can learn, in every instance in which our men galloped into a formed body of the enemy, even if it was four or five times stronger, they invariably routed it, when the French received the attack at the halt.

Conclusion.

I endeavoured in Chapter I. to explain why the French army, which fought so gallantly at Waterloo, was not, and could not have been, "the best Napoleon ever led into the field." Monsieur Thiers, without apparently seeing the effect of his words, in the minds of soldiers at least, gives curious instances of want of discipline in the French Regiments during the battle. His conclusions as to facts cannot be accepted by students who read both sides of the story of the campaign ; but in this particular instance his statements are corroborated by General L'Héritier, who, some years after the battle, told General Vivian at St. Omer that the supporting lines of cavalry, impatient under the losses inflicted by the British artillery, insisted on going forward to endeavour to capture the guns. It was not only in this instance that the want of discipline was shown, but, as Henry Houssaye points out, many years previously, indeed even in the days of Austerlitz (1805) and Wagram (1809), discipline had deteriorated, and in "the Hundred Days" it scarcely existed. The

Rank and File believed, and with some reason, that Napoleon had regained the throne through their suffrages, and, while full of enthusiasm for him personally, they took great liberties with their officers, and still more with the Civil population. We find General Friant, Colonel-in-chief of the Old Guard, complaining that the men refused to accept biscuit as a ration, and that his Grenadiers carried about with them, on the line of march, an enormous quantity of baggage and numerous women.

Napoleon's system of selecting the finest men to be formed into picked battalions has many disadvantages. Shortly after his return from Elba 1300 men of the Line in one garrison demanded to be transferred to the Imperial Guard, and told their officers that unless the transfer was carried out within four days they would effect it themselves!! This desire to join the Imperial Guard was not unnatural, for it was often unduly favoured in the distribution of rations, and, as the rest of the army thought, was seldom risked in an action until the battle was nearly won. Hence their nickname "The Immortals."

All readers of history know the unfavourable opinion the Duke of Wellington expressed of the military efficiency of the army, parts of which fought so grandly under his command at Waterloo; but it is clear that in his adverse criticisms he was comparing it with the British troops he had trained and led for so many years in the Peninsula. There were at Waterloo but very few of those men, some 12,000 in all; but though many of the others were too undrilled to be manœuvred, or even moved more than a few paces under fire, yet the raw militia stood up to die as firmly as did their veteran comrades. Opinions, from so great a general as Wellington was, are often taken for more than the speaker intends. It is true that he described his force as "the worst army ever brought together," and again as "an infamous army, very weak and ill-equipped," but that was in writing to Lord Stewart complaining of the want of support from the Ministry when he first went to Belgium. On the other hand, a fortnight after the battle, when the recollection of the stoical courage of the soldiers was fresh in his mind, in a letter to General Beresford he wrote, "I never saw the British infantry behave so well." A foreign officer, who was present throughout June 18th, quotes an observation of the Duke's as follows: "When other Generals make mistakes their armies are beaten; when I get into a hole, my men pull me out of it."* Nor was this eulogium too high.

* 'Relation de la Bataille de Mont St. Jean, par un Témoin Oculaire.'—" C'est Wellington qui parle : 'Quand d'autres

I have already alluded to the 27th (Inniskilling Fusiliers) Regiment having made a forced march from Ghent. It came under fire about 3 P.M. 698 strong, had 478 casualties, yet never fell back a foot; and Picton's Division lost fifty per cent. of its strength in the two days' fighting.

We know what Napoleon thought of Wellington's Army, for during the voyage to St. Helena, in speaking of the British infantry, he observed, " One might as well try to charge through a wall." No one, indeed, can read the account of how our cavalry charged home, and later, with the gunners and infantry stood up for hours to be shot at, never flinching when their ranks were being decimated, without feeling the deepest admiration for them and their determined Chief.

The conduct of our Regimental officers and men, and especially of the Cavalry, has been generally more appreciated by our foes than by our countrymen. The panegyrics of the methodical Charras may be questioned, on account of his prejudice against Napoleon ; the eloquent passages of Victor Hugo are scarcely accepted in this country, because he avails

---

Généraux commettent une faute, leur armée est perdue, et ils sont sûr d'être battus : quand je me mets dans l'embarras, mon armée m'en retire.'"

himself fully of a poet's licence. There exists, however, fortunately a French opinion of the conduct of our men in the battle, written by Foy, a general who was, as I have shown, one of the last to quit the field of Waterloo, and who was not only a good judge of what soldiers could do, but also a man of the sternest and most inflexible rectitude. He often, in his unrevised diary,* expressed harsh judgments against our countrymen as well as against his own; but his whole life shows that he believed in the accuracy of the statements he made. To prove the value of his testimony I briefly sketch his career.

Foy entered the French army in 1791; he voted against Napoleon's being allowed to exchange the title of First Consul for that of Emperor, and declined to join his brother officers in the address of congratulation on his elevation to the throne. Until the end of 1810, when he was sent to Paris by Massena to explain why he could not carry the Torres Vedras lines, Foy had never met Napoleon, who knew him only as an opponent to Imperialism; but to know him personally was to appreciate his sterling character and great military talents. The Emperor promoted him to be General of Division, and in 1814 had intended to make him a Marshal.

* He died before it was published.

Foy covered the retreat of the French army after the defeat at Salamanca (1812), and stood in the only square which resisted the attack of the German Legion Cavalry at Garcia Hernandez. Elected a deputy in 1819, he opposed the assertion of undue power by the Monarchy with the same firmness with which he had withstood Napoleon's dictatorship.

Therefore, in further explanation of the want of success of the gallant but untrained French cavalry, I cannot do better than conclude these narratives with a translation of Foy's description of the British infantry as it stood unmoved amidst the infuriated hostile horsemen.

"Wounded, vehicles, reserve ammunition train, Auxiliary troops, were hurrying in confusion towards Brussels. The Angel of Death was ever before their eyes, and busy in their ranks. Disgrace lay behind them. In these terrible circumstances neither the bullets of the Imperial Guard fired at point-blank range, nor the victorious French cavalry, could break the immovable British infantry. One would have been inclined to believe that they had taken root in the ground, if the battalions had not, some few moments after the sun set, moved forward in grand array. This they did, when the arrival of the Prussian army showed Wellington that, thanks to his numbers, thanks to his masterly inactivity, and to his knowing how to place his brave men in defensive positions, he had won the most decisive victory of our Age."

INDEX.

ADAM'S brigade, 177
Allied armies, position of, 35; concentration of, 46; at Waterloo, 125
Artillery, march of E battery, R.H.A., 50; Webber-Smith's troop, 73; Major Lloyd's battery, 85, 164; French artillery fire, 156; Allied gunners, 158, 159; French guns near La Haie Sainte, 172

BACHELU, General, seizes Piermont, 76; 183
Baring, Major, 129, 153, 154, 171
Belton, Colonel, 28th Regiment, arrives from England, 84
Berthier, General, suicide of, 22; capacity of, 119
Blücher, Field-Marshal, receives news of French concentration, 46; charger falls on him at Ligny, 62; 175
Bourmont, General, desertion of, 23
British Army, concentration of, 47; without great-coats, 108; French officers' admiration for, 160; courage of 27th Regiment, 172;
Wellington's opinion of, 191, 192; Napoleon's opinion of, 193; Foy's opinion of, 194
British Cavalry, not formed into Divisions, 48; concentration of, 49; arrival of, at Quatre Bras, 98; 7th Hussars at Genappe, 102, 104; Life Guards charge, 105, 106; horses short of food, 108; leaders of, 111; positions at Waterloo, 119, 120; strength of, at Waterloo, 126; at Waterloo, 135-52, 164; French column arrested by, 164; charges of 5th Light brigade, 168; not appreciated by Wellington at Waterloo, 175; brave conduct and heavy losses of Heavy cavalry, 177; charges of Vivian's and Vandeleur's brigades, 178-82; 18th Hussars, 180; squadron of 10th Hussars, 180; humanity of, 181; bravery of an orderly, 182
Brunswick cavalry, at Quatre Bras, 80
Brunswick, Duke of, at Quatre Bras, 77; mortally wounded, 80
Bulow, General von, 46; 65

INDEX.

Bylandt's Dutch-Belgian brigade, 129, 131, 132

CAMBRONNE, General, 8
Cavalry, Continental views of 2; attacking twice in one day, 97; value of, not appreciated by Wellington at Waterloo, 175
Cavalry, see British, French, etc.
Cavalry leaders, qualifications necessary for, 28; biographies of, 111-15; leading the charges, 188
Christie, Ensign, 44th Regiment, severely wounded, 83
Clarke, Mr., 89
Colbert, General, 45
Colborne, Colonel, 52nd Regiment, 177

DELAFOSSE, CAPTAIN, 183, 184; 187
Delcambre, General, recalls D'Erlon, 56
D'Erlon, General, Count, 15; 42; fruitless marches of, 54-8; advance at Waterloo, 127, 128; 131; 183
Domon's division, 16; 40
Dörnberg, General, 48
Duperron, Captain, A.D.C., assists his General, 54

ELLEY, COLONEL SIR JOHN, 106
Elphinstone, Captain, 104, 105
Evans, De Lacy, 137
Ewart, Sergeant, captures an "Eagle," 139
Exelmans, General, 16; his relations with Soult, 17; biography of, 30; advance of, 44; at Ligny, 59, 62

FIREARMS, improvements in, 1, 2
Flahaut, Count, 99
Fleurus, description of country near, 51
Foy, General, at Quatre Bras, 80; wounded, 183; 184; 187; his opinion of British army, 194; biography of, 194; his description of the British infantry, 195
Frasnes, operations at, 45
French Army, efficiency of, 4-8; officers discontented, 8; senior officers, heavy, gross, and incapable, 10; re-organisation of, 10-16; effectives of, 15; concentration of, 15; want of confidence among generals, 17; age of generals, 17; effect of General Bourmont's desertion, 24; disbelief of soldiers, 25; position of, 37; advance of, 38; attack on La Tombe, 40; at the Sambre river, 40; advance retarded by Prussians, 42; divided into two wings, 44; movements of D'Erlon's corps, 54-8; mistrust of officers by the men, 96; hunger of men, 109; apathy of, 118; unwieldy formations of, 142; gallantry of officers, 160; incapability of men, 163; the retreat of, 184; wanting in discipline, 188, 190; biscuit refused by, 191; system of picked battalions, 191; desire of men to join Imperial Guard, 191
French Cavalry, 14; leaders of, 29, 114; advance of, 38; attack on La Tombe, 40; at the Sambre river, 40; advance retarded by Prussians, 42; General Zieten

INDEX.

pursued by, 43; at Ligny, 58–61; at Quatre Bras, 81, 82, 87; strength at Waterloo, 126; at Waterloo, 135; attacks of (3rd attack), 155; confidence of, 158; conduct of Imperial Guard, 163; attack repeated, 164; fourth attack, 165; British line broken by a squadron of, 166; Lord Hill's description of, 167; Piré's threatened attack, 168; causes of failure of, 163, 170; falls back, 170; scare of, 187; want of discipline in, 190
Friant, Colonel, 191

GALBOIS, COLONEL, 92; 97
Genappe, Wellington retires on, 101; sodden state of ground at, 102; 7th Hussars at, 102, 104; position of English cavalry, 103; Life Guards charge, 105; batteries open fire, 107; picquets thrown out, 107; re-capture of British sick and wounded, 107, 108; heavy rain, 108; horses short of food, 108; no greatcoats, 108; French moving on connecting files, 109; hunger of French soldiers, 109; discomfort of French troops, 109; the last stand at, 183
Gérard, General Count, 16; narrow escape of, at Ligny, 52–54; 56; 63
Gilly, operations at, 43
Gneisenau, General Count, deceives the forces at Ligny, 24; 47; orders cavalry to Ligny, 58, 62, 64; his mistrust of Wellington, 72, 175; urges Wellington to support the right rear, 73; 187

Gordon, Lieutenant, 105
Gourgaud, General, 57
Grant, Major-General Sir Colquhoun, biography of, 111; 168
Grenfell, Lieutenant, 105
Groeben, Count, 60
Grohleman, General, 62
Grouchy, General, 43; given command of a wing of the Army, 44; march to Gembloux, 101
Guiton, General, 77; 89

HALKETT, GENERAL, 86; 88; 90
Hamerton, Colonel, 44th Regiment, 83
Henry, Cuirassier, takes a colour, 89
Heyliger, Captain, 107
Hill, Lord, 37; 47; 126; 167
Hobé, General von, 59, 60
Hodge, Major, 104
Hoodwinking of troops, 24
Hougomont, description of, 124
Howard, Major, 10th Hussars, 180
Hubert, General, 80

JACQUINOT, GENERAL, 15; 141
Jeffs, Sergeant Major, 18th Hussars, forcible reply of, 180
Jerome, General, 77
Jürgass, General, 63

KELLERMAN, GENERAL COUNT, 16; biography of, 33; advance of, to Quatre Bras, 87, 89, 90; horse falls dead, 92; flight of his troops, 93; 114; at Waterloo, 165
Kelly, Major, 105
Kempt, General, 132, 133
Kennedy, Colonel Sir Shaw, 156

Kielmansegge's brigade, 84, 85; 172

LABÉDOYÈRE, GENERAL, 55
Lafontaine (General Gérard's A.D.C.), wounded, 52
La Haie Sainte, description of, 123, 124; the attack on, 129, 131; capture of, 153, 171; fire of French guns near, 172
Lance, adoption of, for Light Cavalry, 2
La Tombe farmhouse, attack on, 40
Lefèbvre Desnoëttes, General, 45; 94
Letellier, Captain, pursues Prussians, 60
Letort, General, 43; mortally wounded, 44
L'Héritier, General, 190
Ligny, description of country near, 51; French advance, 54; marches of D'Erlon's corps, 54-58; French driven back, 56; the guard sent forward, 57; French and Prussian cavalry at, 58-61; Prussian guns taken, 60; French artillery silenced, 60; Prussians repulsed, 61; failure of Prussian cavalry, 63; losses at, 64
Lindsay, Major, 89
Lloyd, Major, R.A., retires his guns at Quatre Bras, 85; mortally wounded, 164
Lobau, General, 114; 184
Lüneburg battalion, disorder of, 129, 130
Lützow, Colonel von, captured at Ligny, 61

MACDONALD, MARSHAL, 10

Marwitz, Colonel von der, 63, 64
Maurin, General, 16
Milhaud, General Count, 16; biography of, 29; 60, 62; at Waterloo, 141
Müffling, General Baron von, asks Wellington to concentrate, 47; 147
Murat, General, 18; 114
Muter, Colonel, 136

NAPOLEON meets with 5th Regiment near Vizelle, 8; enthusiasm felt for, 9; his appreciation of the feeling in the army, 9; enters Paris, 10; his disregard of the truth, 25; divides his army into two wings, 44; dissuaded from following Wellington up, 100; 114; capacity of, 115; description of, 116; apathy of, 118; personally directs a battery, 118; on the Rosomme heights, 125; at Waterloo, 141; dragged away from the field, 182; attempts to stop the flight of his men, 183; his opinion of the British infantry, 193
Ney, Marshal, employment of, 25-27; given command of a wing of the army, 44; hesitates to occupy Quatre Bras, 45; moves on Quatre Bras, 75; observations on his operations, 94; ordered to occupy Quatre Bras, 101; 114; cavalry tactics of, 115; sulking, 118; attacks La Haie Sainte, 153; cavalry attacks at Waterloo, 155, 165; at Vieville, 187
Nostitz (Blücher's A.D.C.) assists Blücher's escape at Ligny, 62

O'GRADY, LIEUTENANT, 7th Hussars, 103
Ompteda, Brigadier-General, 171, 172; killed, 173
Orange, Prince of, 37; at Quatre Bras, 71, 74, 88, 90; at Waterloo, 171, 172; wounded, 173, 174

PACK, GENERAL SIR DENIS, demands support at Quatre Bras, 86; at Waterloo, 132, 137
Pack, Major, 144
Pajol, General Count, 16; biography of, 29; 38; advance of, 40, 44; at Ligny, 59, 62
Papelotte farmhouse, capture of, 128
Perponcher, General de, at Quatre Bras, 70, 78
Peters, Captain, 105
Picton, Sir Thomas, arrives at Quatre Bras, 75; 91; at Waterloo, 132; death of, 133; losses in his division, 193
Pigot, Lieutenant, 89
Pirch, General, 43, 46, 65
Piré, General, 16; 76; 168
Ponsonby, Colonel Frederick, wounded, 150
Ponsonby, Major-General Sir W., biography of, 112; 136; death of, 148
Poten, Major, 151
Prussian army, concentration of, 46; disposition of, at Ligny, 51; retires from St. Amand, 63; approaching Waterloo, 174
Prussian cavalry at Ligny, 58-61; reverse sustained by, 58; failure of, 63

QUATRE BRAS, Ney defers occupation of, 45; description of, 66; respective strengths at, 75, 77; Piermont taken, 76; retreat of Dutch-Belgians, 77; charge of 6th Chasseurs, 77; disposition of troops at, 77, 78; charge of Picton's men near Gemioncourt, 79; advance of Foy's division, 80; repulse of the Brunswick troops, 80; 6th Chasseurs isolated, 82; Wellington's narrow escape, 81; attack of Wathier's Lancers, 82; Piré's cavalry retires, 84; losses, 84; French supporting column repulsed by the 92nd, 84; arrival of 3rd and 1st Divisions, 84, 85; Lloyd's battery retires, 85; Pack demands support, 86; Halkett sees Kellerman preparing to advance, 86; Kellerman's advance, 87; position of the English troops, 88; Prince of Orange orders 69th to get into line, 88; Kellerman's charge, 89; Halkett's right battalion takes refuge, 90; 28th Regiment attacked on three sides, 91; Kellerman falls, 92; French become demoralised, 93; losses, 94; observations on operations at, 94-98; arrival of British cavalry, 98; Wellington falls back, 101
Quiot's Division, 131; 171

RAMSAY, NORMAN, Wellington's severity with, 147
Rapp, General, 21
Reille, General, 16; 40; 42; horse shot, 183

P

Re-organisation of French army, 10–16
Rifles, improvements in, 1, 2; probable effect of magazine rifles at Quatre Bras, 98
Röder, General von, at Ligny, 60

SAINT AMAND. *See* Ligny.
Saint Remy dangerously wounded, 54
Sambre river, crossing of, by French, 40; advance retarded by Prussians, 42
Schröder, Colonel, 171
Seymour, Captain, 134
Sleigh, Colonel, commands Vandeleur's brigade, 181
Sohr, General, 63, 64
Somerset, Lord Edward, 103; biography of, 112; 177; 188, 189
Soult, General, 40
Soult, Marshal, his relations with General Exelmans, 17; and with General Vandamme, 19; as Chief of the Staff, 21, 22; 114; 118; drags away Napoleon, 182
Sourd, Lieut.-Colonel, wounded, 107
St. Cyr, General, 10
Subervie, General, 141

THIELMANN, GENERAL VON, 46; 58; 65

UNIACKE, LIEUTENANT, 7th Hussars, gallantry of, 169
Uxbridge, Lord, orders concentration of cavalry, 49; 104; 105; biography of, 113; at Waterloo, 130, 143, 146, 147, 164; leading of, 188, 189

VANDAMME, GENERAL, 16; his relations with Soult, 19; reported desertion of, 24; 38; 42; 43; refuses to obey Grouchy, 44; 56
Vandeleur, Major General Sir John, biography of, 112; 130; 147; 148; 176; 178; 181
Vivian, Major-General Sir Hussey, biography of, 111; 147; 176; 177; 178; attacked by a Cuirassier, 179; leading of, 188

WATERLOO, Wellington retires on, 99; nights of 17th and 18th, 110; Reille's corps advances, 110; biographies of cavalry leaders at, 111; positions of British cavalry, 119, 120; description of British position, 122; Allied forces at, 125; French forces at, 126; hour of commencement, 126; attacks, 127; D'Erlon's attack, 127, 128, 131; Papelotte farm-house taken, 128; position of the Allies, 129; attack on La Haie Sainte, 129; crowding of Donzelot's division, 132; Picton's charge, 133; Kempt's brigade, 133; charge of Household brigade, 135, 141; charge of Union brigade, 136, 141; advance of 92nd Regiment, 137, 138; flight of the French, 138; French batteries wrecked, 140; French losses, 140; French unwieldy formations, 142; French Rear Echelon, 143; British cavalry beyond control, 144, 145; confusion in French ranks, 144; Light brigade charge, 148;

cuirassier spares a trumpeter, 151; retreat of British cavalry, 151; value of cavalry charges, 152; La Haie Sainte- captured, 153, 171; French cavalry attacks, 155, 164; French artillery fire, 156; confidençe of cuirassiers, 158; charge of forty French squadrons, 159; gallantry of French officers, 160; incapability of French soldiers, 163; causes of French failure, 163, 170; conduct of Imperial Guard, 163; fourth attack, 165; squadron breaks through British line, 166; gallantry of French cavalry, 167; charges of 5th Light Cavalry brigade, 168; intensity of French fire, 169; French cavalry falls back, 170; advance of Quiot's division, 171; enduring courage of 27th Regiment, 171, 172, 193; fire of French guns near La Haie Sainte, 172; Ompteda's brigade, 172; fifth attack, 174; approach of the Prussians, 174; value of cavalry not appreciated by Wellington, 175; Vivian moves to support the centre, 176; scene of ruin, 177; Vivian's and Vandaleur's charges, 178–82; troops of the Guard flying, 179; the last stands, 182, 183; Napoleon and his staff, 182; French retreat pressed by cavalry, 182; the flight, 183, 184; French cavalry scared by their own troops, 187; conclusion, 190

Wathier, General, 80, 82, 91
Wellington, Duke of, Army of, 37; asked to concentrate, 47; at the Duchess of Richmond's ball, 48; delay in sending out orders, 48; arrives at Quatre Bras, 71; complains of his staff, 73; narrow escape of, 81; retires on Waterloo, 99; his observation to Baron von Müffling, 148; his despatch, 153; observations on French cavalry, 160; value of cavalry not appreciated by, 175; his opinion of the Army, 191, 192
Wildman, Captain, A.D.C., 49
Wildman, Lieutenant, 105

ZIETEN, GENERAL, 38; makes a stand, 42; retires and is pursued, 43; 47; 65; 99.

LONDON:
PRINTED BY WILLIAM CLOWES AND SONS, LIMITED,
STAMFORD STREET AND CHARING CROSS.

www.ingramcontent.com/pod-product-compliance
Lightning Source LLC
Chambersburg PA
CBHW020813230426
43666CB00007B/995